LEFT AGAIN AT T

The adventures of a middle-aged Dad working at the Glastonbury Festival

To Chris,

with lots of love

Jackie

Christmas 2014

For Big Derek.

WOMBLE 2

The Glastonbury Festival of Contemporary Performing Arts, commonly abbreviated to Glastonbury or even Glasto, is a performing arts festival that takes place near Pilton, Somerset, England, best known for its contemporary music, but also for dance, comedy, theatre, circus, cabaret and other arts.

The festival takes place in south West England at Worthy Farm between the small villages of Pilton and Pylle in the county of Somerset, six miles east of the town of Glastonbury, overlooked by the Glastonbury Tor, in the mystical "Vale of Avalon". The area has a number of legends and spiritual traditions, and is a "New Age" site of interest: ley lines are considered to converge on the Tor. The nearest town to the festival site is Shepton Mallet, three miles (5 km) north east, but there continues to be interaction between the people espousing alternative lifestyles living in Glastonbury and the festival itself.

Contents

Introduction

July 2010

It was about two week after Glastonbury 2010. For some reason-now I cannot remember why- I had arranged to meet Amy in town one afternoon. I know I wasn't in work that day, but I'm not sure why I had the day off. I don't recall why we met in town; possibly she'd had some meeting, or an interview or some training or the like and I was just picking her up. I don't think why we met really matters that much, but it was one of those odd (and few) times when neither of us seemed to be rushing anywhere, so that we could just sit down and relax. Naturally, this involved a coffee.

It was a sunny and warm afternoon and I think it was a Friday. It was so warm that I was sitting outside the coffee shop, cappuccino by my side, ciggies on the go and note book open. I was just beginning to sketch the first notes of what "Turn Left at the Womble" turned out to be. At that time it was just simply a few random words and was intended only to be a sort of a personal diary of what had happened. Merely a record of the year I went to Glastonbury for my first time at 48 years old with my 18 year-old daughter (Amy) and her best mate, Sacha, in tow. It was something to look back on years to come, a "did you really go to Glastonbury, Grandad?" type-thing. I would then dust down some battered old notebooks, dispense Werthers Originals to all and sundry and tell the tales of what I got up to in those Somerset fields, many years ago. They would have thought that I was exaggerating about the horror that was Muse and put it all down to the ramblings of an old man, but I would have known it was all true, and in fact I had spared them the worst. They'd nod indulgently at how I told them that the Flips were the greatest music I'd ever heard. They'd hear stories about Amy that would not be believable. And that's all it was really meant to be- just some notes to look back on. I never really thought it would turn into anything as grand as a book.

That's why it turned out the way it was. I could have made it all sound more exciting than it really was. (Not that it was exciting, but that wasn't really the intention). I simply wanted to record what actually happened at Glastonbury, how it felt and what we actually did. I wanted to give it that whole feel of what it was like, stepping into something unknown, and doing something that I hadn't expected to be doing. By writing it just as a record, and by trying to keep it as matter-of-fact as possible, I knew that it would at least be an honest account of what happened. I could have spiced it up by adding linguistic flourishes or by writing that we did things that never happened or saw things that we never did, but I'd have known that in the future some of it wasn't true. And I'm sure that, over time, I'd have started to blur the line between fact and fiction. I had to have all that build up-the tickets, the planning, the drive etc. Without that context, I don't think that it would have explained how far I'd come as I had when we walked through the gates-both in a geographical as well as a personal sense- since we managed to get those tickets on that Sunday morning in October.

So there I was, scribbling away in my little notebook, Glastonbury wristband still on my wrist, coffee going cold and half-watching the world go by on a sunny Friday afternoon. I was still in that Glasto frame of mind; probably helped by the sun, the fact that I was wearing my shorts and battered sandals and that everyone walking past seemed to be wearing suits and rushing around. I think that it's too easy to get back into that ordinary, workaday frame of mind and that it all can just be a good memory; but somehow I knew that going to Glastonbury changed me. To what extent and in what way I'm still really not sure; I just know that it did. Does all this sound a bit precious, and more than a little bit silly? Possibly . After all, it was just five days at a music festival, wasn't it?

Out of the corner of my eye, I saw Amy come bounding down the street. (That's Amy by the way; she doesn't walk, or run-she *bounds)*. She started waving at me from at least 100 yards away, whilst at the same time motioning for me to get her a drink. I didn't leap into action, I was too relaxed.

 As she reached the coffee shop, she looked at me and then the table quizzically, "And where's my coffee?"

 "I've been waiting for you for ages, it would have been cold. What do you want?" I asked, as she flopped down next to me. (Flops, rather than sits. You get the picture).

"Oh, anything" she said as she nosed into my notebook, "what are you writing?"

"Just a bit about Glastonbury," I replied. There was a slight, imperceptible pause before we both shared a grin.

"It was bloody brilliant, wasn't it?", she smiled.

Chapter 1

A Sunday morning in October

For anyone who has ever gone to Glastonbury, or wanted to go to Glastonbury, or tried to go to Glastonbury, well, you know how this goes. For those who haven't, wanted to or tried to or even thought about it, it goes something like this.

During the preceding months and weeks before the tickets go on sale, you try to put out of your mind the possibility of not being unable to get tickets on the Sunday morning in October that they go on sale. This is difficult because you will have heard over and over again, tales of heartbreak and misery from people who have been unlucky, despite their best efforts (using multiple phones, computers with hyper-fast connections etc-veritable call centre-type operations) and still come up empty handed with no tickets. On the other hand, you hear stories of people who, by using an old PC running Windows 3.1 from a narrow boat deep in the countryside with a dongle internet connection, have managed to get their tickets at 9.01 a.m. on the Sunday in question. Not only that, but they are happily tweeting about having the rest of the day free whilst others are in the depths of despair. So, all this kind of leaves you with the impression that the whole getting-the-tickets thing is not only random and somehow unfair, but that the normal rules of logic, physics and common sense just don't apply. It seems purely down to chance as to whether you manage to get tickets or not.

And because of that, during all those weeks and months leading up to the ticket day, you end up swinging between hopeless optimism and desperate resignation. You'll either feel that it's a given that you'll get a ticket or start making alternative plans because you clearly won't get one. By the time the actual ticket sale day arrives you are in such a state of heightened anticipation that just one cup of decaffeinated coffee might completely tip you over the edge. The nearest thing that I can describe it to is if you could imagine telling a 5 year old on Christmas morning that you have no idea whether Christmas has been cancelled or not; it is simply a matter of luck as to whether Santa has dropped in and left any presents. It may be that his best friend or the child next door has that shiny new bike that they wanted, but if Santa hasn't been to them, well, that's just how it goes. Just blame the elves working for Seetickets at the North Pole. All this causes that Sunday morning in October to be one of the most stressful dates in the year. Adrenaline courses through your veins as if you are running for your life from a very pissed off tiger and in some ways you just want it all to be over, for good or bad.

So, having set the scenario above-which, for all the seemingly dramatic licence, is very close to the truth-in October 2010 it was all very different for me. And not in a good way.

The phrase "spanner in the works" springs to mind when I recall trying to get tickets for Glasto 2011, but, in reality, a whole toolbox would have been more appropriate. I had all the above to contend with, but hadn't accounted for a joker in the pack. On the first Sunday of October 2010 I wasn't even in the country which sort of made things a bit tricky.

We were in our second week of a two week, long-standing holiday in Florida. In retrospect, it was pretty poor planning to be away at that time but what can you do? However much I enjoyed and loved being on holiday with the family and having a great time in America-much better than I could have possibly expected-for just a few hours, I wished that I could be transported back home through some magical Star Trek device to Liverpool, so that I could be sitting at my PC, coffee by my side, ashtray overflowing, phone in my hand and desperately hitting redial and/or refresh in an attempt to get those elusive tickets. But no, I was thousands of miles away; a literal ocean between success and failure, and had therefore had to put a cunning plan into action.

Well, it wasn't exactly that cunning. In fact it was the only plan that I could think of. I'm sure those of a more creative bent or those who could have possibly passed auditions for The Apprentice would have come up with something better than I did yet all I had was to rely upon someone who I could trust to actually get out of bed in the U.K. for 9 a.m. on a Sunday morning and try to get tickets on my behalf. (At this stage, I must add that this was well before I'd written and published "Turn Left at the Womble" and before I'd made loads of contacts through Twitter and the like. Nowadays I know that there are shed loads of reliable people I could have turned to assist me in my hour of need. Back then, however, I was pretty much on my own). Coincidently, and very unfortunately, my two best friends were also abroad on holiday at the time. They would have been the first people I would have turned to but there was no way round it. I was then left with the idea of asking a work colleague to try for me. This was trickier than expected for a couple of reasons. Firstly, everyone I worked with knew of my plight and, being generally a very helpful bunch of folks, most of them wanted to help. Secondly, however, a number of people, quite understandably and although wanting to assist, were a bit wary of what they saw as a bit of an onerous responsibility. This left three or four people who were happy to take the risk and give it a go for me. Instead of asking all of them to try, I decided to just pick one person. Looking back, this may not have been the best tactic. I should have given myself the best possible chance and run it like a mini-phone bank/call centre operation by asking all of them to have a bash at it. Maybe there would have been success in numbers, but logistically it was just too difficult to organise. So I just had to ask one person; someone who I knew I could rely upon but, at the same time, avoid giving offence to everyone else.

That (un)lucky person was Sam, who I'd worked with for ages. Sam's better half worked in IT and had their house totally wired up with hyper-fast broadband; multiple PC's and stacks of mobiles. They had the technology! If they couldn't do it, then no-one could. Additionally, they were those sort of people who were invariably up and about early every morning, even at weekends; so a 9.00 a.m. start on a Sunday would be a piece of cake. (I think that everyone else was quite relieved that Sam had picked the poisoned chalice-it was a bit like the Harry Potter sorting hat in reverse).

Having picked Sam to act as my proxy, I had to explain to her exactly what was required in order to get Glasto tickets on the day they were released. This was difficult to do without edging into hysteria. I didn't want to appear too pushy or to put too much pressure on her; but, on the other hand, I had to stress that it wouldn't be just a case of picking up a phone or logging on at some arbitrary point some time on the Sunday morning in question. It was a case of getting the balance right. I also had to tactfully suggest that it would be good if she was ready to roll on the dot of 9.00 a.m. i.e. fully awake and not hung over from Saturday night! I knew that I was asking a lot (and expecting a bit of a miracle anyway), but I was sure that if anyone could come up with the goods in my absence, then Sam was the one. So with every confidence in her and having reassured her that if it didn't work out, then I knew she would have tried her hardest, I armed her with all the practical details. I planned this like a quasi-military campaign. I had typed a sheet of instructions-phone numbers, URLs, registration numbers etc. Tips about opening as many browsers as possible on as many devices as were available and hitting redial on the phones over and over again. I think that I even laminated the typed sheet that I gave to her. Everything was in place. It was simply a question of waiting until that fateful Sunday and hoping that she would strike gold. There was nothing more that I could do. I went off on our holiday to Florida, knowing that when we came back Sam would have been in touch to tell us that Operation Gettickets had been a resounding success and that it was all down a combination of my meticulous planning, her sterling efforts and the gods looking down kindly on me. I just knew that on that long flight back across the Atlantic, I would be whiling away the hours by planning in my head what I would be doing that following June in Somerset.

So that Sunday was exactly half way through our Florida trip. I'd been sort of putting it all to the back of my mind during the first week, trying not to tempt fate and just getting into the holiday mode. It had been a great holiday, but on the Saturday night, I did go to sleep thinking what the next day would bring. We were planning to go on a bit of journey on the Sunday, so it was an early night for all. I drifted off with visions of pitching our tent in the sun.

Bearing in mind the time difference between the U.K. and the U.S., (5 hours behind the U.K), I knew that when we got up, then good news would be in the offing. Not being very good with mobiles/texting in any way, shape or form, I was reliant upon Sam texting Jackie with the update. At 6.00 a.m. U.S. time Jackie got a text that Sam had sent at 9.30 a.m U.K. to say that she was on and trying but with no success so far. No worries-there was still time. I got up, made a coffee and paced up and down with a ciggie, like an expectant father. Next text- Sam had still had no luck but was still trying. She kept updating us and I knew that the next text would be "Yes!". But at 7.15 a.m. a text arrived- "Oh I'm so very sorry, no luck, it's all sold out". When Jackie told me this I honestly thought she was joking in that sort of "I didn't get the job/pass the exam" crestfallen-face but "No, I did actually!" way. She wasn't joking at all-it's not the kind of thing you joke about. And whilst I was eternally grateful for Sam and knew that she had given it her all-that was it -no Glasto in 2011.

I tried to let the news sink in, although I still didn't really believe it. I did ask Jackie more than once if it was really true, if she was joking and if Sam had really got the tickets-even though I knew it was a false hope. I did half think that we'd get another text from Sam saying she'd somehow managed to get a ticket and it was all a mistake, but after an hour or so I had to face up to reality-there were no tickets and all the efforts had been for nothing.

It was a bit of a grim morning that day. The drive to the theme park took an hour or so and I didn't feel too jolly. Jackie kept saying all she could say, things like "Well, there was always a risk you weren't going to get tickets" and "You know Sam will have tried her best" as well as "Don't get too down-hearted, these things were maybe meant to be" alongside "At least you had a great time in June, maybe it just can't be repeated". All this was meant to make me feel better and was said with the very best of intentions, but it didn't really work. I was too pissed off and dejected. A lot of shrugging and nodding went on. I was trying to say that I understood and that I was ok, but inside I was metaphorically kicking the cat. Not that we either a) have a cat or b) if we did, that I would kick it or even consider it, but that's the way with metaphors-I was in that sort of kick something around frame of mind. It wouldn't have meant that I would have actually ended up with tickets or made me feel any better yet for a bit that's how it was. At the same time however, I did feel both a bit guilty and selfish for feeling that way in any event. Jackie had said that I shouldn't let it spoil my holiday and she was totally right. It was true that the experience of going to Glasto in June could never possibly be repeated anyway and I just had to develop that stiff upper lip British attitude. After all, I was in America at the time and that is what us Brits are renowned for. So I manned up (as our American cousins might say) and put it all to the back of my mind whilst I sobbed inconsolably into my sugar coated U.S. cereal breakfast.

No, I didn't actually shed any tears even though I felt like it. We headed off to Busch Gardens along the interstate (motorway) with the sun blazing down and had a pretty good day after all. There were a couple of occasions (albeit briefly) when the frenetic activity slowed down for a few minutes or so, and I found myself thinking "Oh fuck it. Bloody Glastonbury tickets" but those were few and by the end of that day I had resigned myself to the fact that I wouldn't be going to Glastonbury in June 2011. I'd probably see more on the TV anyway -and at least I could say that it done it once. Some magical experiences in life are only destined to happen once anyway.

Chapter 2

This was the Winter of my Discontent

The flight back from America after the holiday was a killer. Not because I was still grumping about not being able to get tickets for Glastonbury, but just because it was at such an ungodly hour and jet lag had kicked in. I'd only ever flown to the Med before going to the U.S. so this eight hours malarkey was a bit of a novelty. On the way out it was fine; start of a holiday and all that excitement/adrenaline it brings. On the way back home, then it was a completely different matter. I think that the flight was late in day so we were all tired in any event, fed up that a brilliant holiday was over and not exactly looking forward to getting back home. On top of it all however, was the niggling thought at the back of my mind that I would be going back home without the promise of Glastonbury to look forward to the following June. I don't think that I mentioned it on the flight back but it was just there, like a nagging toothache; no tickets for Glasto. Everyone was so pissed off with the journey, the thought of being back home and going back to work that, for once, I was fairly sensible, and didn't mention I was in a much worse position than everyone else because I didn't have Glastonbury tickets. If I had done so, then there was a fairly high probability that I would have been thrown off the plane. Mid-Atlantic. With no parachute. But nevertheless, during the whole journey back, I was kind of miffed that my plans of planning the Glasto trip in my mind had fallen at an early stage.

On returning to work the following week I was, in a blindly optimistic sort of way, thinking that Sam might be waiting with an e mail telling me that she had, in fact, actually got hold of tickets for me and the whole thing was an elaborate practical joke cooked up between Jackie and her. I could have forgiven both of them easily for that and would have seen the funny side of it. I knew in my heart of hearts that it wasn't going to play out that way, but maybe one percent or half of one percent of me thought there might be that possibility. But as soon as I saw Sam that Monday morning I knew it wasn't going to be the case. She couldn't have been anymore apologetic and I felt so guilty for feeling sorry for myself. I said to Sam that it didn't matter and that I knew she'd done all she could; it was a lottery really and that I was simply grateful that she'd tried. I genuinely meant it (all except the part about it not mattering). It did matter-but I couldn't tell her that. I just shrugged in a "that's ok" way and went and made everyone a coffee.

So this was at the end of October, and however much I tried to put thoughts of Glastonbury to the back of my mind, it was nigh on impossible. I had resigned myself to the fact that I wouldn't be going and didn't hold out any hope at all for the resale. I rationalised it all by knowing that I'd had such a great time in 2010 and maybe, in a sort of stoical (yet Eeyore-ish) way some things are destined never to be repeated. Each time anyone asked me, in all innocence, whether if not I was going to Glastonbury again, like the aforesaid Eeyore, I mumbled something about not being able to get tickets and went back to my metaphorical default position of standing in the corner of a field, morosely chewing thistles. I also worked on a premise of the line-up probably turning out to be crap and the fact that I'd save so much money by not going. All this was completely hollow of course and didn't ring true, but I had to do something just to stop from getting completely obsessed by it all. (Not about being obsessed about Glasto per se; I think that the boat had sailed on that one, but being obsessed simply about not getting tickets). It didn't exactly help that I was still writing "Turn Left at the Womble" and therefore memories of 2010 were naturally to the fore. Similarly, I hadn't shut myself off from music entirely-that would have been a step too far. This did however mean that I kept reading about Glastonbury, seeing rumours about who would be playing, listening to recordings from 2010 and above all, still clicking on websites that I'd bookmarked that had anything vaguely to do with Glastonbury, "just to see what was happening". It was sending me bonkers. Sometime mid-December, and probably because Christmas was looming, I decided enough was enough. I determined to put it all behind me and just to concentrate on the tasks at hand i.e. work, the annual madness that is Christmas, surviving the miserable weather and doing all the usual stuff.

December (and Christmas, by extension) came and went as it always does. The weather turned really nasty in January and unusually for us in Liverpool, we ended up with thick snow on the streets and ice that remained stuck for at least a fortnight. At this stage, getting the 4 miles or so to work every day was a higher priority than even thinking about getting all the way to Somerset in June. In all senses of the words, Glastonbury seemed many miles away.

But, in a narrative twist that was always going to happen, through that truly miserable winter weather there appeared the faintest ray of hope. Somewhere along the way there was that glimmer; and for the life of me, I cannot exactly recall how, when or where this precisely happened. Sometime in January, I stumbled across the fact that there were a number of charities advertising for staff to work at Glastonbury. This may have come through an e mail, the Glastowatch forum, somewhere on Facebook or possibly in some sort of blinding flash of internal inspiration. The latter is extremely unlikely. Whatever way it was, I discovered that two charities were recruiting bar staff. I personally haven't many readily transferable skills, having worked for the major part of my career as a civil servant, but another string to my bow-in fact the only other string on my two stringed instrument, is that I worked in a number of pubs for a good few years. I was therefore, in theory, an ideal fit for the role. This is what I told both Shelter and the Environmental Justice Foundation (EJF) when I filed an application with them. What I didn't say was that although I'd had seven or so years experience of pulling pints, it was about 20 years ago that I'd last stepped behind a bar. I was hoping that it was like riding a bike and that I could just wing it. After all, the drinking culture couldn't have changed that much. I guessed that it was all still pints of bitter and glasses of Makeson. Maybe pints of Woodpecker if the punters were feeling particularly adventurous. Or even the odd Snakebite or bottle of Babycham. Something along those lines.

Being a natural-born pessimist, I didn't really expect much to come of these applications. After all, all it entailed was dropping something on line and it wasn't exactly the most taxing application form I've ever had to complete. Even more so, I figured out that there would be hundreds of people applying for just a few jobs and even if they weren't already all sewn up through networks of mates, then with my luck in getting to Glastonbury for 2011 I thought I'd still end up sitting at home come June, watching it on BBC and cursing under my breath.

January came and went. February is always a miserable month anyway and the snow, ice and generally dreadful weather didn't seem to want to go away. Looking back now, I can say that nothing memorable happened at all. It was simply a matter of watching the calendar count down and holding out the hope for better weather. I was still glimpsing at all the websites about Glastonbury every so often, but in reality I had given it up as a bad job. The sites for both Shelter and EJF weren't telling me much either and I didn't expect to hear from them again. One afternoon however, at the end of March, I went for a coffee during a late lunch. I only had half an hour or so break and then weather must have got a bit better, as I was sitting outside the coffee shop, enjoying a cappuccino and having a smoke. I did have my Kindle with me and after reading a bit of the book that I was currently on, I thought I'd have a brief glance at my e mails before heading back into work. As the page loaded, I nearly fell off my chair in surprise. I certainly dropped my ciggie and knocked what was remaining of the coffee (luckily, only a drop) all over the table. There it was. An email from EJF nestling amongst the usual assorted rubbish, telling me that "Congratulations! You have been selected to volunteer at Glastonbury on behalf of EJF!" I did a quick double take and I hadn't been dreaming, the email was really there. Was it spam? It certainly looked genuine-there was a whole agreement thing to sign and instructions about what to do next. I quickly read it and scurried back to the office, where I read it again, in a bit of disbelief to be honest. I had to determine if it was actually from them or if was some sort of scam, so after reading it through one more time, I phoned them up on some flimsy pretext. I can't exactly remember what I said, but I do recall thinking that I shouldn't ask anything too spectacularly daft. After all, I didn't want to blow it at the first hurdle. Luckily for me, I must have come up with something both vague yet not ridiculous enough to make me appear totally unemployable. It all turned out to be genuine; it wasn't some scam or ruse to extract money under false pretences; it was the real thing, and probably my best and only chance of getting to Glastonbury in June 2011.

It turned out that the exact way it worked was like this. Well, not exactly as that would be a bit boring, but the rough way was relatively straightforward. EJF asked for volunteers to run a bar at Glasto. In turn for a fee to them (this is where the charity bit came in), they supplied these volunteers to an event company called Avalon who actually ran the bars, supplied the drinks and infrastructure etc. Avalon appeared to a lot of this for Glastonbury, for many different charities (including Shelter, from whom I had heard diddly-squat). EJF, Shelter and Avalon were all vetted/contracted by Glastonbury and were all reputable. (Being a bit paranoid, I didn't want to end up as a victim on Watchdog or ending up sold into some sort of white slave racket. Even worse, I could have been forced to spend the rest of my working life as a roadie for Muse. Can't be too careful). But they were all ok and the practical side was that all I had to work three 8 hour shifts over the weekend in return for a free ticket. Piece of cake. Only 3 shifts. And it wasn't like really hard work, just serving a few drinks. (Oh, how naïve was I? More later).

I did have to come up with a deposit of £200 in advance i.e. equivalent to the ticket price, that would be refunded to me after the festival and once I'd done the shifts ok. I guessed that that was fair enough, it stopped anyone just getting in under false pretences. On a practical side, there also appeared to be distinct advantages in working the festival, rather than going as a punter. (I would soon be in a position to use that awful word "punter" as opposed to "crew". Neither of which sound wholly correct when spoken in any accent that is remotely Northern. I will attempt to not use them at all in the rest of the book, but if I do, then it will either by accident, rather than by design. Or in an ironic sense. Whichever way it, may I apologise in advance?) The practical advantages for the "crew" (ha!) was that they would be camping on a roomy site with 24 hour security and no access for anyone else. Free transport to and from the festival by coach from a number of selected (yet unspecified) points across the U.K. There would be free meals -breakfasts and hot foot, cooked by "professional" chefs. It did make me wonder somewhat when the term "professional chef" was used. As opposed to what, exactly? Amateur chefs? The mother of someone who worked for EJF who could rustle up a few plates of fish fingers and chips if required? Never mind, fish fingers and chips would have been alright as far as I was concerned. There would also be hot and cold running water and hot showers-open 24 hours per day! It sounded so good that I couldn't really see many downsides.

So, like joining the Foreign. Legion, I signed up on the dotted line (including my £200) and I would be heading off to Glastonbury in June, with not much of a clue about exactly what would happen or what lay in wait for me. It was really like dipping my aged and wrinkly toes into totally uncharted waters.

Chapter 3

Kind of Getting Serious

I woke up the next morning after signing on the dotted line to wonder if it had all been a dream. Had I imagined it all? Was I actually going to be going to Glastonbury in just 3 months time? Switching on the PC and checking my e mails confirmed that no, it wasn't simply something lingering in the sleepy recesses of my mind, but that I had committed myself to working a bar somewhere on the site. Blimey. There was a lot to sort out in a matter of a few weeks.

Luckily, I already had booked leave off from work for two weeks either side of festival, so I didn't have to go grovelling at a time when getting time off would have been at a premium. I hadn't cancelled the leave so maybe in some deep sub-conscious way, despite my outward pessimism, I knew that the ticket gods would eventually smile on me, one way or another. (But maybe they would turn out to be old-school gods, malevolent and nasty, with a trick up their sleeves for me somewhere along the line?)

Whichever way it was going to turn out, there were many things I needed to do. Or rather, many things I needed to get hold of. Following our inaugural trip to Glasto the previous year, we had ditched most of the stuff I needed to camp. Tent, ropes, groundsheets, chairs, sleeping bags; they'd all gone. In an ecological sense I would very much like to say it was because they had been well-worn and served their purpose well. This is not strictly the truth however. Some of the stuff was, indeed broken. One of the three chairs we took wouldn't stand up properly and one of the cases that we carried our gear in was knackered beyond repair; ripped and torn, with one wheel hanging on, the rest having shed themselves in some kamikaze fashion as we dragged it across the whole site. But that was it really. The sleeping bags, tent, ropes, groundsheet and other assorted equipment were all perfectly serviceable and in an awful admission I have to own up to the fact that we bundled them up, put them in bin bags and threw them in the bins. Now I realise as I am so much more aware and so much older (well, I'm now 51 and then I was a mere 48 years old) that leaving almost everything there goes against the whole "love the farm, leave no trace" ethos. However, we just couldn't face lugging it all back up the hill of death. There was just too much stuff and although I suppose that the tent would have been just about ok, it had taken a bit of a battering and I'm not completely sure if it would have stood up to the rigours of another Glastonbury; especially if there was going to be any rain. At least we didn't just leave everything where it was and walk away like so many others did (and still do)-we did tidy it all up, and all that was left was a patch of flattened grass. Small consolation I suppose and not something I'm very proud of.

So what this all meant was that I had to virtually start from scratch in getting what I needed together, in a relatively short period of time and without wanting to spend a ridiculous amount of money on everything.

I searched for everything that I had left from the previous year and sized up the whole nature of the issue. It was a pretty poor show. It took me all of about 10 minutes to gather it all together. I still had a little camping stove, kettle and mug. Two little torches; one of which seemed to have been switched on for a year which had resulted in the batteries leaking some evil acid-y type goo. An emergency foil blanket. (Why did we have this? It wasn't as if I was planning to run a marathon). One camping chair. Two unopened and unused plastic rain ponchos (which I'd got free with a magazine, so I wasn't exactly confident in their rain-repellent qualities). And that was it. Apart from my wellies, which luckily hadn't been worn at all in 2010 as the weather had been so good. I had so little stuff in total that some careful planning was needed. A list was required.

I knew basically what was required, but didn't need any excuse to go over-the-top and look on the internet. After half an hour so or I had two lists. The first was all the big, essential stuff and the second was all the little, essential stuff. The former list had all the very obvious things that were needed-tent, sleeping bag and rucksack. (The first time we went I made the mistake of thinking that we could use any old sports bag/suitcase. Not a good idea). On top of this I added an air-bed because although using a big duvet the previous year worked ok, it was cheaper and seemed more appropriate and not as amateurish. And that was it. The second list had all small to carry and cheaper items; guy ropes (wasn't very confident with these as we didn't bother with them the year before), tent pegs, sleeping bag, new torches, blow up pillow as well as all the consumable things such as toilet roll, medicines, biscuits and the clothing that I didn't have (long welly socks) etc. For all that it may seem that going to Glastonbury is a bit of a haphazard, hippy experience; throw things together and sleep in a ditch or under a hedge-I am always surprised at how much people generally get it all together and how professional they are. (There may well be more of this later in the book). Because of copious notes and guidance that EJF/Avalon had mailed me since I'd signed up I decided against lugging the camping stove as free and limitless coffee seemed to be available on demand. That would do for me. I never used the stove for anything else than boiling water anyway.

So come the end of April (payday) and with only a matter of six or seven weeks to go we headed off one Saturday morning to shop with the lists in hand. For once, and possibly the only time ever in my life, the shopping trip was a success. So much so, that by one o'clock we were sitting back in the car, eating fish and chips with everything on the lists ticked off, bought and stowed in the boot. It was all going swimmingly.

One of the final pieces of the jigsaw that needed to put into place was deciding exactly how I was going to get there. I had either the option of driving or going on one of the free coaches. There were advantages of driving myself; I could determine my travel time with a bit of flexibility and I could go from door to door (well, door to tent) myself without having to mess around getting to the coach. I would also be able to take much more gear with me if I drove rather than having to carry everything with me on a coach. On the other hand, the car wasn't 100% reliable and I would need to let it have a bit of a mini-service before I drove all that way. Additionally, I had to factor in the cost of fuel, which would have added up to a fair old chunk, driving all the way from Liverpool to Somerset and back again. And that would have been enough, even before I would have got invariably lost and therefore spending much more on fuel than any calculator on the internet told me it would be. It was like one of those pro- and con- things.

There were distinct advantages about the coach though. I wouldn't have to be concerned about traffic and if the car was going to get there in one piece. If I was knackered on the way back-which I knew I would be-then I wouldn't have to worry about falling asleep at the wheel; I could actually get my head down and have a proper kip. I'd also be travelling with people who I would probably be working with; it would give me a chance to meet some of them beforehand-and, in any event, feel part of the whole thing. The downsides of the coach were really the same as the upsides of using the car; I'd have to get to wherever the coach was going from and get dropped off there at goodness knows what hour on the way back. My flexibility and independence were therefore limited.

Also limited was exactly what I would be able to take. I'd have to be able to carry everything I took by myself, without any assistance from Amy and Sasha (my two little sherpas from 2010). Not being exactly the fittest chap in the world, this presented a bit of a challenge. Would I be able to carry a heavy rucksack as well as my tent and everything else? Was some pre-Glasto training necessary? The answers to these two questions were "Christ only knows" and "Yes, but I can't be bothered-I'm too far gone". It was fairly evenly matched between the car and the coach. It did cross my mind that Avalon didn't give much info about getting there by car. I rang them and after a few lengthy but helpful conversations I managed to wangle myself a car park pass if I needed one. They still didn't know where the coaches were going from; there would be one from London (no use) and another, somewhere "up North" but they hadn't exactly decided where. It all depended on where the majority of the volunteers were travelling from. They doubted there'd be one in Liverpool, but I guessed that Manchester might not be a bad bet. (I was a bit sceptical about their geographical grasp as well. "Up North" was a bit too vague, and having dealt with these London types before, it could have meant anywhere from Birmingham up to Edinburgh.

I do realise that this is a bit of sweeping generalisation, but having spoken to someone earlier this very week from London who thought that Newcastle was about 10 miles away from Liverpool, then you can see where I was coming from. That isn't a one-off either). I therefore had the option to drive if I wanted and was, to use an unfortunate turn of phrase, veering in that direction. I decided to wait until a bit nearer the time until I knew more details about the coach.

The remaining time before Glasto sped by without really noticing. Before I knew it, it was the beginning of June and therefore only 3 weeks away. Apart from buying all the gear a few weeks before, I hadn't done anything else. I knew that I had to try to put the tent up, in a practice run sort of way, but considering my general ineptitude in all matters tent-related, I'd kept putting off the evil day, but faced with such a short deadline, I knew that I'd have to face up to my demons and just do it. At the very least, if there was something missing or broken, then I'd have time (just about) to sort it out. I couldn't really leave it until when I was actually at Glastonbury to try to put it up for the first time. (As a side issue, and this is something I've noticed every time I've been to Glasto, is that everyone else seems to be an expert at putting tents up. Even really complicated, big ones seem to get whizzed up with no difficulties and look really professional; tight, florescent guy ropes and everything securely in place. Each time I've put our tent up, it's always involved a lot of wrestling and swearing, and the end result appears to look as if I haven't a clue about what I'm doing or really know how it should turn out. Which I haven't and I don't. The fabric always seems gravitate towards slackness, so by the end it's the camping equivalent of some wrinkled prune. Whereas everyone else's remains as tight as a drum, repelling water and wind, without a second thought). Anyway, I decided I couldn't leave having the practice run any longer, so one night after work I summoned up the courage to give it a go. Now for ease we'd got one of these new-fangled pop- up tents, which in theory, should be able to be erected with simply a deft flick of the wrist. I was a bit sceptical about this. Surely this was the camping version of the old "whip-the-tablecloth-off-whilst-leaving- the-bone china-in-place" trick. It would all end in tears. Always ready for a good laugh, the whole family gathered around while I studied the instruction booklet intently. It did seem fairly simple and because it was only a two-man tent, I decided not to mess around with putting it up outside. The front room would do. It was a flat circular affair when packed; like a big nylon pancake. I undid the packaging, and to my utter surprise, it seemed to leap out of my fingers of its own volition and jump into the middle of the floor, all set up.

"And you all doubted me", I said, somewhat triumphantly. "I knew exactly what I was doing".

Amy looked at me, over her cup of tea. "Ah, you've just got to get it all back in place now. That should be easy as well."

Sarcasm is not a very likeable trait in one so young. We all looked at the tent in its glory and the unanswered question was how on earth was I going to be able to return it to the basic 2 dimensional pancake shape without something breaking? There was a pause whilst I said I needed to study the instruction booklet-a fancy name for a slip of paper with instructions that made no sense at all. Everybody knew that it would be a miracle if I managed to get it back the way it was supposed to be. There was a longer pause whilst I very kindly offered to make everyone a brew. This was not done with any altruistic intentions really; it was simply a way of buying myself a bit more time in the hope that either a) everyone would get bored and wander off or b) they'd all nag my father-in -law, who, being much more practical than I am, to put it away in my absence. Unfortunately, neither of these two things happened.

I walked back into the front room with everyone's drink, to find them all perched on the edge of the sofa, craning their necks over the top and side of the tent so they could still watch the TV and acting as if was the most usual thing in the world. The only things that were said were, "Do you know what to do now?" followed up by, "You're going to have to do this all by yourself at Glastonbury, so we're not going to help." (This sounds a bit unreasonable in print, but I think that it was said with the best of intentions at the time). The difficulty I had was that as the whole thing shot up by seemingly by magic and without any assistance on my part in seconds, so all logic and reason about simply reversing the process was irrelevant.

The instruction booklet seemed written in a way to personally baffle me-as if it was written specifically with someone as cack-handed as myself in mind. It had a sneering tone, with liberal use of the word "simply" and line-drawn illustrations that made as much sense if I looked at them upside down and in a mirror than the right way up. I wouldn't have been wholly surprised if it had started with, "Dear Rick Leach, Thank you for buying your tent from us. Here are the instructions showing you how to put your tent back together. These have been written in a way a 5 year old could do it. With one hand tied behind their back. However, you don't stand a chance you thick bastard. Why don't you just throw it away and hire a camper van? Yours sincerely etc". It worried me a bit when the booklet talked about "bend pole A over pole B" with guidance of "crossing hands over" and "take care not to force the poles". I could see it ending up with many tears and shards of fibreglass scattered around the room. Everyone one else was, in reality, looking forward to a right old laugh and being able to recount hilarious tales, many years hence, of the time I had to be taken to hospital with a self-inflicted injury involving yards of cheap nylon and tent poles.

I looked out of the corner of my eye. Amy's fingers were hovering suspiciously over the 9 button on the phone and everyone seemed to have lost complete interest in the latest goings on in Coronation Street. There was no way round it. I was going to have to grab the metaphorical nettle and the literal tent and just have a go. According to the booklet, it all could be (and had to be) done in one manoeuvre. There was no room for pussyfooting around. "Right," I said, "Stand well back, here I go." There was a dramatic pause and everyone held their breath (or stifled their giggles; not exactly sure which) as I grabbed both sides of the tent, twisted my arms and wrists in a style destined to cause something to dislocate in my lower back, and somehow managed to return the tent to the flat semi-circular shape in one fell swoop. I really don't know how I manage to do it; it was more by accident than design. Without waiting for the collective round of applause that was surely warranted, I whipped it back into the cover and triumphantly zipped it up. I bowed to everyone and was ready to give my speech. I could sense a slight air of disappointment that it all had gone so well. "Bet you wouldn't be able to do it again," said Amy. Although I was tempted to rise to the challenge, I thought that once was enough. Next time I'd be doing this would be in a field in Somerset, surrounded by people for whom putting up a tent is the most natural thing in the world.

Once I'd mastered the skill of getting the tent up, I was nearly all the way there. Well, not actually there at Glastonbury, rather that one of the major hurdles had been negotiated. The next thing that I had to decide on was how I was going to get there. I prevaricated a long time over this until it really came to the point of no return; it was getting too close to the date and unless I made a decision I would lose out on the chance of either a car park pass or getting there on the coach. Having weighed everything up, it did really make more sense to get the coach than to drive; at least I wouldn't be shelling out for the price of fuel.

I still hadn't heard much from Avalon about the coach, so I ended up ringing them to find out what the score was. They were really helpful as usual, but the news they gave me left me with a bit of a logistical headache. The good news was that they had laid a number of coaches on; some from London (obviously) and some from "up North". And therein lay the problem. London was clearly not an option, but the "up North" one wasn't exactly simple either. I hoped against hope that it was Liverpool or even Manchester, but no, it was leaving from Sheffield. Now, I suppose in their defence that most places north of Birmingham are vaguely in the same geographical area and that in any event, it would have been a bit much to lay on coaches from every major city in the North, but it would have been slightly easier for me to get to Manchester than to Sheffield. But that's what I had to do and told them it was ok and said that I now didn't need a car park pass. Everything was falling into place and they'd send me an e mail with all the details.

When I got home from work that night I did indeed have an e mail from Avalon; in fact there were two emails, as well as one from EJF. Things were moving at some pace.

The mail from EJF was inviting me to take place in some fundraising event for them prior to Glastonbury; as much as I felt that I should (both on moral grounds and as a matter of self-interest as well), as it was happening one evening the following week in London then it was impossible for me to get there, because of work as much as anything else. I dropped them a mail right back, full of apologies and in an air of paranoia wondered if for some odd reason if it would, even at that late stage, preclude me from getting to Glastonbury. Would I end up on their "naughty list"? Would knocking this back mean that I might end up getting my deposit returned and ending up watching the festival on the BBC? I vowed to phone them the next day, just to make sure.

The mails from Avalon were a bit more practical. The first one did indeed have all the details of the coach; where it was going from; timings and the like. The second one was a bit out of the blue, and something that hadn't been mentioned in any of the numerous phone conversations I'd had with them up until then. It was titled "Training" or something along those lines, and was all about a "familiarisation event" that was scheduled prior to the festival. Again, and not wholly unsurprisingly, this shindig was taking place in London the following week. Now, if there had been a way I could have got there I would have done, but it there was no way I could have got the time off work. Well, I could have at a push, but getting to London at such short notice wasn't exactly a cheap experience. All this warranted another apologetic e-mail and further questions in my mind as to whether it would mean I'd stumble at the last hurdle. I half-expected an e mail to pop back into my in box saying that "Due to you being unable to complete the training, we regret that..." etc. But there wasn't, although I went to bed in a bit of a pessimistic frame of mind.

Back in work the next day, the first thing I did was ring EJF to allay that particular issue to rest. To my relief I realised that I had been worrying unnecessarily; they weren't bothered one jot and I had a really good chat with them; they were more concerned about whether I'd got everything I needed from Avalon than if I went to their fundraising thing . This made me feel even more guilty that I couldn't be there and I wished that there was a way round it. Nevertheless, I then had to ring Avalon to find out about this training thing. The more I'd been thinking about it overnight, the more I'd convinced myself that this training was an essential prerequisite for the job and without doing it, then everything would fall apart. In retrospect, I don't really know why or what lead me to think that way; there had been nothing from Avalon that explicitly stated that training was mandatory; there wasn't even anything implied that would have made me assume that to be the case. However, as I picked up the phone and dialled them with some trepidation, I knew that the Glastonbury dream for 2011 was due to come to an abrupt end.

Having been in touch with them a few times, I did have a contact name and a direct line which made it slightly easier.

"Hello, Alice, erm, I'm ringing about this mail you've, erm, sent me about this training thing for Glastonbury," I stuttered, as if I'd never used a telephone before.

"Yes? And how can I help? What do you want to know?" she replied.

"Well, it's just that, erm, I can't, well, umm, actually get to London next week, y'know, work and stuff, and I'm a bit worried if it would be difficult for me if I couldn't be there," I rabbitted, wanting to appear concerned enough to understand the clear importance of this training, yet, on the other hand, not wishing to come across as a bit of a neurotic and obsessed crazy person. I had visions of her grabbing a marker pen, striking my name off a list and passing a note to a colleague as we spoke, which read "Not a chance. Take him off the list. Barmpot."

"No, no," she replied, "It's all fine, it's just some optional get together, really for anyone who is around and available in London next week. We wouldn't expect anyone to make special arrangements for this."

"Oh, but the mail mentions the word "training", and I thought.."

She laughed, "Sorry, that's my fault. I was typing the e mail really quickly and couldn't think of a better word to put. Sorry if it's misled you. It's not training as such; you'll get all that at the festival. It's really a chance to explain what happens, how the shifts and bars work, a chance to meet up with the bar managers and for any questions to be answered."

"Oh, I see," I said, "That makes sense, I was just thinking that if I couldn't make it, then it might be, erm, a bit of a problem and you might not need me." I half-laughed, as if this was the daftest thing ever, whilst thinking to myself that if she'd just worded the e mail better then I needn't have gone through all of this. Having said that, I was looking at my pc at that very moment with work e mails coming back to me, because I had been totally unclear on something. I'd had managed to set off a chain reaction that was wholly unwarranted. People in glass houses etc. But there was really no problem , explained Alice, there was no real need to be there and I needn't have worried; she was sure I would be fine with my vast experience of bartending. I kind of agreed in a non-committal way, as I didn't want to give away the fact that the last time I stood behind a bar and served any drink was about twenty years ago. Probably if anyone could do with a bit of training it was me. "Oh, have you got my other mail about the coach?" I asked. There was a bit of a tapping of the keyboard in the background.

"Yes, that's fine, not a problem again," said Alice. "Are you ok with getting to Sheffield?"

"I think so, I'll sort a way out. Sorry to have messed you about with the car parking and all the rest." I had no clue at all about how to get to Sheffield; in fact I wasn't 100% sure where in Yorkshire it was-which was a bit ironic, considering I'd tarred everyone from London with the same brush.

"But did you get all the other stuff I sent you?" she asked, "Did it all make sense?" Now I had got the other mail which she'd sent me although I'd only sort of glanced at it; I'd not printed it nor spent any time going through it, but I said that it all was fine and that it covered everything I needed. (As I said this, I opened it up and printed the whole thing so as least I'd be able to read it later in the day). Because I'd spent the last 20 minutes basically chatting on the phone, whilst pretending to get some real work done, my work inbox was filling up with stuff as I was talking. As good as it was I decided that I should really concentrate on the day-job and said goodbye and thanks to Alice, in somewhat a better frame of mind than before. I couldn't really spend the rest of the day dreaming about Glastonbury, could I?

But I could and I did. It was all too easy to get distracted, and I kept glancing at what I'd printed earlier, skim reading it while I was on the phone, trying to do the usual work day stuff. The only way to describe pre-Glasto stuff to someone who's not been is that it's sort of like going on holiday; you're counting down the days, but in a subtly different way. When you're going on holiday, you do have a vague idea of what to expect; with Glastonbury, there is a similarly vague idea. However, holidays do tend, by and large, to end up quite close to what you've anticipated; each time I've been to Glastonbury, it's always been so been so completely and utterly different that there's no point trying to second-guess what will happen. This is not me trying to over-romanticise the whole thing- I don't want to fall into that trap, but I simply think that there are so many variables at play regarding Glastonbury that it can never turn out the way you anticipate.

All this didn't stop me day-dreaming about it all however. I was switching between over-hyped excitement at the whole thing and thinking that it would be even better than the year before and truly nervous about the prospect of stepping into the unknown. There were so many aspects about the latter that at times I found myself thinking, "Oh my god, what the fuck have I done, signing up for this?". When I looked at it in the cold light of day, I was probably right to be a bit tentative. I would be going by myself. I would be doing a job that I hadn't done for 20 years and one which I wasn't sure I could just pick up at the drop of a hat. I would travelling on a coach from a city I didn't know with an actual coach load of people I didn't know. I would have to put up a tent all by myself. I didn't have my little sidekicks, Amy and Sacha with me-and at the very least, because of that, would have to carry everything by myself. That was irrespective of the fact that a major part of the sheer enjoyment of the previous year was that we were all in it together and in many ways a shared experience is something to be treasured. I didn't know what the weather would be like; and if it was bad, how well would I cope? After all, in 2010, it was so hot and dry that the only time we saw our wellies was when we packed them to go and when we packed them to come back. The worst that they had to cope with was being stuck at the bottom of the tent, silently forgotten about and gently being covered with a layer of fine dust. Everyone who hasn't been-and a fair few people who have been-go on and on about "the mud". Would I able to cope with that? I was really unsure on that point. And because I was going on the coach, rather than my own car, if it actually all turned out to be a disaster then I wouldn't be able to just up sticks and bugger off home early. I would kind of be stuck there, marooned in the mud or whatever for a week.

However, despite all these feelings of doubt (and they were real, I'm not exaggerating at all with the intention of any artistic licence), I knew instinctively that everything would turn out fine; largely because Thomas told me, in that manner only your 21 year-old son can do, to "man up". (Not sure about the inherent, implied sexism of that instruction, but I knew what he meant). Secondly, it wouldn't be the most difficult thing I'd ever done; how hard would it be to spend a mere week there whatever way it turned out to be. Finally, and most importantly, I knew that if I bottled it then I'd regret it; not just today, but tomorrow and for the rest of my life. I'd always have Glastonbury. (I know I shouldn't have watched Casablanca again last night before writing this). It would be an experience, for good or bad, and as there is only one chance in life to do anything different, then I shouldn't let it pass me by.

Armed with all this buzzing around my head, I headed off on my (early) lunch with the printed guidance from Avalon in my hand to give it a proper read and to make sure I'd covered everything.

While I had skim-read it before, as I sat down with a coffee at the café, I gave it a good going over. A lot of the information was generic to going to Glastonbury anyway and really was a list of do's and don'ts. Or rather a list of what to take and what not to take. Although I had a clue about what I needed in general for going to Glasto, having the previous years experience as well as advice from various websites, it was good to have it all down in one place. Especially as it was printed rather than in my usual indecipherable scrawl. There are always a few useful tips of things to take that may make all the difference, but probably what is much more useful is what not to take. The "less is more" aphorism is something that definitely applies when going to Glasto; it's just a pity that I've never really stuck to it myself. Every time I've been I've always taken stuff that I've never needed or used or just forgotten about until it's time to pack up. My ambition is to travel there with just a toothbrush and a tent.

What Avalon told me I did had to take, which was different from the previous year, was photo id, simply just so they knew who I said I was. This was fairly logical I suppose, but it did mean taking either my passport or driving licence; neither of which I fancied losing in the mud at Glasto. An alternative they suggested was the "Over 21" photo id card thingy that the young folks use so they can get served with a drink. Don't think that would have worked with me. I don't need a photograph to prove that I'm actually over 21; years of drinking too much coffee, eating not 100% healthily and smoking way too much has given my skin a leathery sort of complexion that only can be truly rivalled by Keith Richards. So it was my either my passport or my driving licence. People always say that the photographs on their passports are dreadful and imply that they don't look as horrific in real life and in 3 dimensions. I can honestly say that the photographs of myself on both my passport and driving licence are amazingly accurate however, and for that reason alone I couldn't see anyone wanting (or able) to pass themselves off as me. But I had to take that proof of identity otherwise I wouldn't have got in. (Luckily, Avalon mailed everyone a further missive a few days later, saying that photocopied passports etc would be fine, so I suppose other people had had the same reservations as myself).

The other things that they told everyone to take related to uniforms. I knew this because there was a section on the e mail headed "Uniforms". I didn't expect this. I hadn't seen anyone at Glastonbury the previous year wearing anything that could be considered uniform- like, except for police officers for whom I suppose that uniforms sort of come with the job. But Avalon were telling me about uniforms. When I read the relevant section, what they were saying was that there no uniforms were required (which was a relief) but that that we were expected to wear plain, dark t-shirts when working. I thought that would be no problem, but it was only when I got home that night and checked that I realised that I didn't actually own any plain, dark t-shirts. It's not as if my wardrobe was full of gaudy, fluorescent 80's type clothes, it was just that none of my shirts were dark. Plenty of plain white ones, but nothing dark. So it warranted a little trip to Asda and the purchase of five of the cheapest black t-shirts they had. (All of this is fairly unremarkable and a bit boring, but please bear with me. The t-shirt issue will crop up later).

So it was only about two weeks to go and I was nearly all sorted. After a bit of to and fro-ing I had arranged for my brother-in-law, Robbie, to drive me to Sheffield for the coach pick up. I had toyed with the idea of the getting the train (or even a coach) there, but getting a lift was in some ways the easiest option. Thanks to the marvel that is Google Maps, I'd printed out directions and searched for the exact point where we had to get to; an arts centre/student union thing named the Hubs; which was right in the middle of the city. Ironically, it turned out that the Hubs was virtually across the road from the train station; certainly you could see the station from the Hubs so it may actually have saved a lot of messing around if I had got the train. But the car it was and I ran through both the maps I'd downloaded with Robbie as well as sitting down at the laptop and going through Google Street view, so that he would know exactly where we were going and that we wouldn't get lost at all. He said that he knew how to get to Sheffield very well, having driven there on many occasions and that the city centre was so small, that there'd be no problems. So that was all right then. Travel and timings were sorted out; we had to be there for at 7.00 pm on the Tuesday night which meant that with a mid- afternoon journey down the M62 we'd miss most of the rush hour. Looking back, I should have cottoned onto the fact that if we were leaving Sheffield for Glastonbury at 7.00, then we'd only be getting to Glastonbury after midnight. I'm sure that Avalon told us that; and even if they hadn't logic would have dictated that would be the arrival time. Whether I'd fully appreciated that or not, probably because I was that elated to just to be going, seems slightly daft in retrospect as I hadn't understood what a late arrival would entail. But that's for later on. At that moment all travel details were in place.

The last week or so in work went with a bit of a blur. I kept looking on the internet about Glasto and picking up information from forums about what it was like working there. One person in particular was very helpful, having worked it for years and years, and sent me loads of useful stuff; hints and tips, photos and the like. He was especially helpful about protocols in bar working; cash handling and watching out for scams. It had been so long that I'd worked a bar that although I thought it might be a bit like riding a bike, a few pointers didn't go amiss. It had also been so long that I'd actually gone for a drink in a hip bar (not that I ever have, I don't think), that I had a quick chat with Thomas and Amy to discover what new-fangled drinks the kids were having these days. I didn't want to appear hopelessly out of touch after all. They weren't really much help. I'd like to think that they had an unshakeable faith in their Dad being able to serve any type of drink and that I would be the master of the bar; but it was more of a shrugged "what are you worried about?/you'll be fine/thought you were making a brew/pass me the remote" type conversation. I just think that they didn't see it as a big issue-I was racking my brains as to the types of drinks I used to serve; bitter, lager, mild, cider. Babycham and Cherry B. It was that long ago. I decided just to wing it and see what happened.

I finished work on the Friday before. Two weeks off. One week working and one week to recover. As I left work on the Friday evening, my work colleagues wished me all the best. I'd like to think that they were slightly jealous of the marvellous opportunity I had; they were probably thinking however that they were glad it was me rather than them and that I kind of taken leave of my senses. I might have been fairly competent at times in respect of my day job, but serving drinks to thousands of people in a muddy field Somerset was possibly beyond me. I didn't have to be an expert on reading body language to see that was the general expectation. There seemed to be a fair bit of sympathetic smiles being bandied around and more than one person said something along the lines of, "Hope you cope with all the mud ok; bet you can't wait to get back behind your desk!" All this sounds a little harsh and more than a bit paranoid really. Looking back I'm sure that everyone actually thought I'd be perfectly alright with it all-it's just that my confidence wasn't the greatest.

The weekend was spent, in part, with packing and unpacking the rucksack, making sure I had everything. As usual with me, numerous lists were involved which meant that I kept ticking things off as I packed them into the rucksack and then wondering if I really did or if there were stray, phantom ticks popping up. I'd rummage around in the rucksack to double- and even treble-check if I had put in the tiny torch for example, or the packet of painkillers even if they'd been already ticked off. What didn't assist was Thomas winding me up with, "Are you sure you packed xx or yy, or have you ticked the list in error?" and then laughing as I went through the whole rigmarole over and over again. His best jape was telling me that he'd thrown a few ticks on the list himself while my back was turned; and then telling me that he hadn't really or maybe he had and that the only way for me to be sure was to start all over from scratch. After toothless threats to disinherit him from all my worldly fortunes, he decided to stop pissing around and help me with my logistical nightmare. It really only took half-an-hour or so to get everything in the rucksack and in some sort of fashion that allowed me to get essential stuff out easily. I hoisted the whole thing onto my back and very nearly crushed a number of vertebrae. "I'll be alright if I don't have to walk too far with it," I gasped, "Give me a hand getting it off." I knew it would be lighter on the way back because by then I would have eaten the packet of ginger nuts stuff in the side pocket.

So that was it. Everything was in place and everything that could be done had been done. I went to bed on the Monday night knowing that the next six nights I'd be spending under canvas. Well, not canvas as much as lightly water resistant nylon. As the alarm clock flicked from 11:59 to 12:00, my last thoughts before I dropped off were that this time tomorrow I'd be in a whole different place.

Chapter 4

On The Road

On the Tuesday morning, one of the first things I did was check the weather forecast for Glastonbury. I don't really know why I do this so much in advance; it is a cliché, but you can't actually change the weather. What will happen, will happen and all you can do is prepare for, if not all, then most eventualities. And I did have most things in place; wellies, coat, cheap rain poncho, hat, suncream, brolly. (I knew that the list would come in useful). The only weather forecast that I feel you can wholly rely upon is what's on the BBC. There's a myriad of other longer term forecasts (21 days, 28 days in advance); but they are not worth a carrot. They are all based on some sort of trend analysis mathematical formula based on previous years weather, rather than actual Met Office science. But it didn't stop me looking at them for weeks in advance, which lead me to veer dramatically between ridiculous optimism, "See, it's going to be 25 degrees every day with no rain so I won't need those wellies", to hopeless pessimism, "It's going to rain every day the week before and all through the festival. And there are going to be gale force winds with a possibility of snow. Have I got a balaclava anywhere in the house?" There was one forecast that I glanced at, about three weeks before, which predicted that the temperatures in Somerset were going to range between 7000 and 8000 degrees Celsius during the festival. Either there had been some sort of data entry error at their end or the Eavis' had decided to relocate the festival to the surface of Venus. At least that would give the fields a proper chance to recover. So the only forecast that could be relied upon with any sort of credibility was that from the BBC. And that was telling me that it would a bit of a mixed bag. Fine and dry (yet overcast) on the Tuesday/Wednesday, but then the dread, woolly phrase of scattered showers for Thursday/Friday. It would finally be topped off with a bit of sun on the Saturday/Sunday. It didn't sound too bad. Scattered showers for a couple of days. It would only be a bit of light, summer rain. I could handle that. In fact, it might provide a slight bit of welcome relief. After all, it was a bit uncomfortable the previous year with that intense heat every day. At that stage, ignorance was indeed bliss. I had no clue about what a touch of "light rain" would do.

As I stuck my head out of the front door however, it looked pretty good. I'm not one of those weather-beaten old country coves who can predict how things are going to turn out weather-wise simply by looking all gnarly and wise, sniffing the air and sticking a finger in the wind, but everything seemed ok. The sky looked like one of paintings that only a 5 year old could come up with. The sky was bright, bright blue and because it was sunny, all the clouds had that brilliant white fluffiness to them. Like little balls of cotton wool. On the downside, it was fairly windy and those cotton wool balls were scudding across the sky at a steady pace. This was a tad alarming. It was warm however and certainly it didn't warrant wearing a jacket or a sweatshirt; which meant that they had to be crammed into the already bursting at the seams rucksack. But that was the weather just in Liverpool; it may have been a whole lot different in Somerset. The only way to check for sure was to look on the BBC. Bit of a circular way of doing things. In general all this messing around with the weather counted for squat. I just had to get there and cope with whatever it threw at me.

I pottered around in the morning and made sure there'd been enough calories consumed to keep me going for a fair old while i.e. a big breakfast and an early dinner. Robbie turned up to take me all the way to Sheffield mid-afternoon and after loading the car and saying my goodbyes to Jackie and Amy, off we set. It did feel very odd going without Amy, as she had been such an integral part of the whole thing in 2010. Not just odd, but a little sad as well; but she couldn't come and that was it. Thomas had decided to come along for a ride, so there was safety in numbers. We were only going to Sheffield after all. (The safety in numbers bit is nothing to do with the inhabitants of Sheffield; it was more to do with the fact that Robbie can talk for England. Any distraction from incessant chatter was to be welcomed and Thomas coming along for the ride provided that outlet. Lest I be misunderstood in any way at all, I feel I must really mention that I was very grateful for Robbie giving me a lift as without that I'd have been at the mercy of public transport. It was rather that just sometimes silence really is golden; but the other side of the coin was that if Robbie did chatter all the way to Sheffield and back then it would have stopped me worrying unnecessarily about what would happen at Glasto). A prime example of this was that even before we reached the end of our street-which is only short- I asked Thomas to check if I had actually remembered to put the tent in the boot. I had, but that didn't stop me from cross-checking. Robbie's chatter therefore would keep me from continually going through such ridiculous rituals.

The journey was quite straightforward and quick. We headed along the M62 to Manchester; a road I knew very well, having to use it to go to work three times per week. It was easier driving along it mid-afternoon than during the rush hour. The imminent threat of death due to psychotic drivers seemed to be less than usual. Before we hit Manchester itself we turned off and followed the signs to Sheffield. Everything was going swimmingly, even when we turned off the motorway and followed the A-road. Robbie said he knew the route very well and time wasn't a factor, so it was a bit dispiriting when, driving through a village, he suddenly applied the brakes quite hard, did a u-turn and swung round to go back the way we came. "The roads have changed since I was last here," he said, somewhat unconvincingly. I looked at Thomas and shrugged. The road and houses looked as if they had been that way for a couple of hundred years. It wouldn't have wholly surprised me if the local natives were clattering down the roads wearing clogs and on their way t'mill (as no doubt they say in those parts). No, there didn't seem to be any new roads at all but as we were being guided by Robbie's expertise we had to trust his judgement. Thomas had a blinding flash of inspiration and suggested to Robbie that the signpost directing us to Sheffield might just help a bit. A touch of mumbling combined with a hasty three-point turn and we were literally heading back in the right direction.

We zoomed along the road and never having been in this part of the world before, it was quite a knockout. Across the moorland, the road hugged the edge of the hills, snaking and twisting. I don't really class myself as a full-blown city person, but I was staggered at how quickly we had left the outskirts of Liverpool and Manchester behind us and where now in what I would term wilderness. Not in any sort of Alaskan-type-nothing-for-hundreds-of-miles-surrounded-by-bears, but it is all relative I suppose. At one point I looked out of the window and all I could see were miles and miles of rolling moorland. There wasn't a house or any building, not even a barn or shack, to be seen. There weren't even any sheep grazing on the hills. Although we had a clear view of the road ahead and behind us, there were no other vehicles. I looked all around and the sky seemed immense. We were totally alone in what appeared (to me) to be a vast wilderness.

But, it was never going to last. Before I wax too lyrical, we were only driving between Manchester and Sheffield. It wasn't as if it was some road trip through the outer stretches of the mid-west or the deserts of Mongolia; I haven't checked, but I think that there's probably only 35 miles or so between the two cities. People drive that far in America just to go for the shopping, the pictures or for waffles at the local diner. Something along those lines. It would be waffles wouldn't it? Apple pie and ice cream? So it wasn't a Kerouac On the Road thing and my coffee was still warm and drinkable in the travel mug I'd brought with me.

We were soon driving down hill all the time. We'd hit the top of the hills and Robbie pointed out Sheffield in front of us, nestling like the promised land through the windscreen. We started to pass farmhouses scattered at the side of the road, more and more frequently as well as a couple of big reservoirs. The farmhouses were gradually replaced with ordinary houses and we started heading into what was clearly the edge of the city. Robbie started to shift a bit uneasily in his seat.

"What's the matter?" said Thomas "Are you alright?"

I rummaged around for the printed maps and directions, thinking that Robbie was winging it and didn't really know where we were going.

Thomas asked him again, "Rob, are you ok? Do you know where we are going?"

"Yes, yes, I know where to go. See, there's the signs for the city centre."

"Well, what's up then?"

"I just need a piss. Keep your eyes open for somewhere."

"You just keep your eyes on the signs and the maps. We'll watch out for any toilets for you. Don't get lost."

Like driving into any city, you had to keep up with the traffic, which was fairly busy. On top of this, there seemed to be a myriad of speed cameras, bus lanes and one way systems. If you lived in Sheffield itself, then it would have been very logical, but as outsiders we were having to make quick decisions about which lane to be in at any one time and which signs to follow. This resulted from my poor map reading and what must be said, Robbie's fast and erratic driving. Other drivers on the road must have been cursing us and indeed, on more than one occasion, a horn was sounded as we moved across three lanes of traffic to take a sudden left turn.

"Robbie," I said, "Just slow down a bit and take your time. It's not a race. We're miles ahead of time.

He looked a bit agitated. "I am absolutely bursting. Have you seen anywhere yet?"

Being more concerned about staying in one piece and trying to understand the map, finding somewhere for him to empty his bladder hadn't been at the top of my list. I turned around to Thomas in the back.

"I haven't seen anywhere," he said.

All this conversation took place as zoomed down a hill towards a set of traffic lights, cars, lorries and white vans either side of us. Suddenly Robbie swung the wheel to the left and undertook everyone in the bus lane. There wasn't even enough time to ask what he was doing. Another left turn and he bounced into a car park of a building that was part of the University of Sheffield. We knew this as he nearly hit the big sign outside as we screeched to a halt. He leapt out of the car, Starsky and Hutch style and bounced up some steps into the building. An elderly security guard tried to stop him, but all we could hear was Robbie saying, "Sorry mate, can't stop" as he run past him, in a fair imitation of Usain Bolt. Thomas and I looked at each other, open mouthed. There wasn't much to say.

Five minutes later, Robbie emerged from the building, looking much more relaxed than previously.

"What the fuck was that all about?" I said. "You can't just walk into any old building and use their toilets."

"Oh, it was ok," he replied airily, as if he did this sort of thing all the time.

"But didn't security stop you?"

"No, he couldn't keep up and anyway I darted into the first toilet I found."

"Anyone else see you?"

"There were a few people around but I just nodded to them as if I worked there and they let on back."

It was good to know that the one of our institutions of academic learning, and a medical one at that (we could tell that from the nearly demolished sign), was safe from any potential terrorist who could just wander in off the street, relatively unchallenged. Or from a 40 year-old Scouser in desperate need of relief.

"Come on," I said, "Let's get out of here before you get the car clamped." He'd parked willy-nilly in the parking area, blocking at least three cars in. As we eased out of the car park back onto the road, Thomas alerted us to what was happening in our wake.

"Look at that security guard," he said.

I turned around to see the old bloke come hobbling down the steps after us. He was only short of waving a stick at us and shouting about "pesky kids" and it would have been a scene lifted straight out of Scooby Doo. I knew by now that we were not on the right road, but must have been fairly close to where we were supposed to end up.

"Robbie, you don't really know exactly where we are do you?"

"Erm, sort of, I've got to kind of, erm get over by there." He waved his hand in a vague direction.

"Look," I said, "You're never going to find it and we're going to end up on a one way system going the wrong way. Pull over and let's ask someone for directions."

With that encouragement ringing in his ears, Robbie managed to bring the car to a halt from 40 mph to zero in a remarkably short amount of time. Leaning out of the window, he managed to quickly attract the attention of the nearest pisshead who was wandering around the ring road in Sheffield that afternoon, and who, unsurprisingly had a) a bit of difficulty in understanding Robbie's accent and b) a bit of difficulty in understanding anything.

"This is hopeless," said Thomas, "Try to find someone else."

We looked around and there was a taxi parked about 20 yards from us. I took the maps from Robbie (who was still trying to discuss the finer points of geography and navigation with someone who was clutching a warm can of Tennants) and ambled along the pavement towards the taxi.

It only took a couple of minutes for me to understand from the cabbie exactly where we were and exactly where we needed to be. More importantly, and quite ironically, whilst we weren't literally within spitting distance from our destination and none of us could throw a stone too far, we were within walking distance. In fact, if we had craned our necks and squinted, we could have seen it on the other side of the ring road. However, it being a one way system, it was a bit tricky to negotiate and I had to stop Robbie from haring off again at a tangent.

"See, this is where we are," I said, stabbing my finger on the map, "and this is where we have to be. The cabbie has said that the best way is to do a u-turn at these lights and then take the second left down the side road. It'll be right in front of us."

"I knew that," Robbie protested, "I'd worked it out. You needn't have spoken to him."

Thomas raised his eyebrows (yet again). As much as I knew that Robbie hadn't worked anything out, didn't know where we were and didn't know how to get to where we had to be, there was no real point in arguing further with him. It was easier and less stressful to let him believe that thanks to his map reading abilities and his skills in discussing utter bollocks with one of Sheffield's prime time drinkers that the situation would be resolved. Robbie knew that as well, but would never admit it. He followed my (or rather, the cabbie's directions) to the letter and within less than five minutes, we had shipped up outside our destination.

It was an odd building, all curves and glass, and contrary to what I expected, in total darkness. I anticipated it to be a hive of activity, with a massed line of coaches waiting to take us to Glastonbury and throngs of volunteers milling around. It was eerily deserted. I could understand that the building itself was closed; it was part of the University and being that all the students had gone home for the summer, I guessed that there wasn't much call for the Students Union to be open. Naively I had presumed that there might have been some sort of check-in type thing however, with possibly free coffee, pastries and croissants being served for all the volunteers. But there was nothing. There wasn't even much traffic moving up and down the street. It was like the way city centres used to be on Sunday afternoons. There was no reason for anyone to be there. A few cars were parked up but there were no pedestrians around.

"Are you sure this is the right place?" asked Thomas, echoing what I was thinking, "It's all a bit quiet."

"I think so. Look, here's the map and here's the photos of it from the internet. It is where we are supposed to be. Maybe it's so quiet just because we are so early."

We were early as well, even after all the messing around, getting lost and unscheduled "pit-stops", it was still only a little before 4.30. i.e. over two hours before the coach was due to set off. This left a bit of time to kill before I hit the road properly. Thomas and I wandered over to the train station, which was a few hundred yards away and came back to the car (and Robbie) with all manner of food from Burger King. "You may as well get going," I said to them, "I don't really want you to get stuck in all the rush hour traffic." If the truth be told, I would have rather that they had waited with me until I was on the coach and on my way, but being 49 years old, it didn't feel wholly appropriate to by waved off on the bus as if was my first day at school. Although I had a bag with me, it wasn't exactly my first satchel and I didn't have my dinner money tucked into my socks. I hadn't heard any stories of the big boys picking on the little kids, but I did know that the toilets were grimmer than anything any school could have ever thrown up at me. (An apt phrase in context, I suppose). Thomas said that they would wait to see me off, but as soon as they had finished their assorted burgers, fries and catering-sized drinks, I could see that Robbie wanted to hit the road again. I had no doubt that the journey back for Thomas would be as eventful as it had been on the way there, but that would be a whole other tale. For now, it was really time to say my goodbyes. I gave

Thomas a hug, said my thank-you's to Robbie and grabbed my rucksack from the boot. It would be good to write that I swung it over my shoulder in a sort of happy-go-lucky-carefree-wanderer style, but it was closer to oh-shit-this-so-heavy-how-on-earth-am-I-going-to cope-with-this-and-what-is-that-strange-cracking-sound-in my-back. Still, I waved them off with a fixed smile and waited until the car turned round the corner and out of sight, before I collapsed on my knees with the sheer weight of the damn thing.

Once I had regained my limited composure, I wandered into some sort of arts centre/gallery/bar place next to where we had parked, ordered myself a coffee and sat by a window, looking over the road to the Hubs, waiting for the arrival of both the massed coaches and throngs of volunteers. I wasn't actually waiting that long, maybe 15 minutes or so, before cars started pulling up and dropping off student-y looking types with their rucksacks and assorted gear. I decided to stay where I was for a bit, finish my coffee in a relaxed manner and suss everything out before I staggered across with my rucksack.

It didn't take much time before the pavement was filled with clumps of these young folk and assembled heaps of tents, bags and the like. I scanned the whole scene with a view to seeing if there was anyone remotely close to my advanced years as everyone seemed to be about the same age as Thomas, or even a bit younger. I didn't want to be the only person on the coach over thirty. It would have felt a bit odd. Luckily, I did catch a few glimpses of some receding hairlines and faces that looked a bit more lived-in than the fresh-faced youngsters, so I realised with a sense of slight relief that I wasn't going to be in a minority of one. It must be said however, that pony-tails mixed with grey hair and baldness are to me, are a big warning sign of tragic hippy-ness. Throw in tie-die and it makes me want to revert to my punk roots and drag my old leather jacket with covered in Crass badges out of the wardrobe.(I never actually had a leather jacket but you get the point which I'm trying to make). On the other hand, if I had to spend five days in the company of either a bunch of students or old hippies, then I probably would feign an interest in the collective works of Gong and the Grateful Dead.

I finished my coffee, heaved my rucksack onto my back and nearly decapitated a number of Sheffield's distinguished contemporary art lovers with my tent as I negotiated my way to the door. Mentally flashing peace signs to the hippies, I crossed the road just as a coach ambled up the road. One coach, not a fleet. A coach. In the singular. This would be it then. Everyone that was here on this one vehicle.

A slightly older, school-teacher type figure then appeared on the scene, as if by magic, complete with the obligatory clipboard and megaphone to corral people into some sort of order. She was accompanied by a sidekick, who was clearly was there to do all the fetching and carrying. "Hello, everyone!" she breezily announced. "My name is Sarah and this is Donna," pointing at the assistant. "And we're from Avalon. We're going to be with you all the way to Glastonbury. I hope you are all working for us at Glastonbury and not expecting a holiday somewhere else!" I think this was her attempt at humour. "If you could all get your papers and i/ds ready and let Donna know who you are, then we can be on our way as quickly as possible. " I fully expected her to tell everyone to make sure they'd had a wee before they got on the bus but she didn't. Just like it is at the airport when it's announced that the flight gates are open, there was a bit of a mad scramble as people rummaged in their bags and pockets for their papers and surrounded the already clearly overworked Donna, wanting to be the first on the bus. And, like at the airport, I couldn't really see the point. They would have got on the coach, come what may, and no one seat is better than another. However, there would always be people like that and I let things die down a bit before I had my credentials checked and ticked off. The coach driver, who couldn't have been or looked more coach driver-y if he'd tried, (tight white shirt stretched over a fairly expansive waistline, the first three buttons undone; slacks, slip on shoes; gruff yet jovial; a fish out of water a bit with all these scruffy types; a penchant no doubt for wholly inappropriate jokes and comments) was helping everybody load their stuff in the cargo bit on the coach (don't know if it's called that, but luggage hold sounds not quite correct either). With an almost balletic skill that belied his appearance, he grabbed my rucksack and tent and swung it deep into the bowels of the coach. Armed now only with my little backpack, I climbed up the steps and into the coach. I gave myself one last look around at Sheffield before I made my way down the aisle and settled down into a seat by the window, fairly near the front. "This is it," I thought to myself, "This really is the point of no return. Glastonbury here I come."

Whilst I had made pretty comprehensive notes during my Glastonbury trips and have quite an accurate recall (I think) of things that happened, that coach journey was and still is, all a bit of a blur. Maybe it was because it had been a long day already or that it was quite simply just a tad boring, but there are only fragments of it that come to mind. Whereas the rest of this book is crammed, you may think, with inessential details, this part will be sped through in a few brief paragraphs. I would like to go into it minute-by-minute, and hour-by-hour, but there's just nothing that really springs to mind, however hard I think about it.

The noteworthy details-or really the only details I can remember are a bit jumbled up and a bit fuzzy. I do think that I fell asleep at some point in the journey; motorways have that effect on me, but most of the time thankfully when I'm a passenger, rather than when I'm driving.

What I do recall is the following; the coach wasn't completely full because no on-one was sitting next to me. That was a good thing because it meant that I could stretch out and have a bit of space, and also fall asleep. (Which, for the purposes of this book, is not a good thing I suppose, and has led this bit to becoming a tad sparse). There were a group of about six or seven girls about Amy's age (19/20-ish I guessed) in the two rows of seats directly in front of me who didn't stop talking all the way down to Glastonbury. In fact, as the journey progressed, they grew louder and louder. I do realise that by writing this, it does make me sound like a grumpy old man, but I'm not really like that. It didn't bother me at all and all I'm trying to do is recite what it was like. Seated immediately behind me were a couple who seemed quite, well, I think "posh" is the only way to describe them and were seemingly a bit like fishes out of water being on a coach from Sheffield.

But they were ok and I exchanged a few words with them on the way down. The coach driver did the usual coach driver stuff-making jolly japes over the microphone and telling us when and where we would be having a leg-stretch and a toilet break.

The only thing that I was keeping an ear out for was what was going to happen with shifts and other practical arrangements. It must have been a fair way into the journey when Sarah (who was sitting in the front seats of the coach; just like teachers used to do on school trips) stood up and announced over the coach P.A. system that we would shortly be told what shifts we all be working. I don't know for sure, but I bet that she had a pair of glasses on a cord round her neck which she balanced, precariously, on the end of her nose. She was that sort. Poor Donna clutched a bundle of papers which were handed around the coach. It was like something FIFA would have devised for the Champions League draw, but poorly photocopied. We all ended up with a single sheet of paper showing groups arranged alphabetically A-J. These groups showed what shifts people would be working and at which particular bars. It was all slightly academic as none of this told us which particular groups we would be individually assigned to. This required a different sheet of paper that was handed around. It wouldn't have surprised me if Donna had produced a Perspex globe form which she had produced numbered balls and had the coach driver announce the names, football draw style. But it was only when this second sheet of paper was distributed that we could really see the full implications. A wave of silence moved throughout the coach as everyone studied the two sheets of paper, matched themselves up to the right group and worked out exactly what they would end up doing. This silence faded away and was replaced with shouts of delight or dismay as everything sank in.

Looking at the two sheets of paper I could see the three shifts I had been given. The first was Thursday 11 a.m. to 7 p.m.; that was ok. The other two were evening slots; 7 p.m. to 3 a.m. and two consecutive nights; Friday and Saturday. There were some immediate downsides with this. Because of the line up that I knew about this meant that I would miss out on seeing Coldplay and U2; probably the two artists that I wanted to see more than any others. (My innate musical conservatism coming to the fore at this point I think). It also meant that two of the major nights would be wiped out with working. Maybe it was because it was the first time that I worked that I ended up not having a weekend day shift, but I wasn't sure. Maybe it was just the luck of the draw. At that precise moment when it dropped to me what I'd be working I was more than a bit pissed off. All that planning and I would miss out on the two big nights. I would have, at that time, been quite happy swapping either of those shifts for the Sunday night as I wasn't at all interested in seeing Beyonce, who was the Sunday headliner. That's how I felt at the time but as it turned out, like most things in life, Glastonbury has a way of surprising you in unexpected ways. I'm not so fatalistic to just go with the flow every time and see what happens; that is simply a way of being at the mercy of others' whims; however, in this instance, that is what I decided to do and in many ways in retrospect it was the best choice. I did still think at that point that I'd possibly try to get someone I was working with to swap a shift, but determined that it would be easier to do it when I'd sussed out the lay of the land. The only other thing that was evident from the sheet was that I'd be working at the Cider Bar. I had absolutely no idea what that entailed; it sounded like it could be busy, knowing what I knew about cider and Glastonbury. But that was the extent of my knowledge/guesswork. It was a cider bar at Glastonbury. Could have meant anything. It was more the shifts that concerned me; three nights and two of them at the very times I just didn't want to work. Bastard. But...that's the only way I could have got there anyway, by working, so I had to take the rough with the smooth. All around me on the coach, and particularly in the seats in front of me, there was a general hubbub of excitement as sheets and lists and shifts were compared. It all seemed a bit irrelevant to me because I had the impression that none of them had ever worked in a bar before or indeed worked at Glastonbury. They were in for a bit of a surprise I thought to myself. I didn't realise how much of a surprise I was in for however.

The only other things that I recall about the journey was stopping off at a service station at about half past nine where I think I must have had a quick bit to eat, a coffee and a smoke (because that's what I do) and it starting to rain just a little bit. As soon as it had started, it stopped, so that wasn't much to worry about.

As the journey progressed, and I kept drifting in an out of sleep, I was mildly astonished to find it becoming dark. Why exactly this took me unawares, I don't really know. After all, I had been told that we could be arriving late at night, so the idea of turning up when the stars were out shouldn't have been wholly unexpected. Maybe it was because we had turned up in bright sunshine the previous year. However, as the coach progressed on its merry way along the M5 and as I woke from fitful sleep to see dusk turning into night through the windows, I was slightly startled. But no more than that. I hadn't grasped the full implications of what that would mean when we did finally arrive.

As the coach turned off the motorway, I knew that we were getting close to the promised land. I tried to visualise and memorise the route that the coach took so that it would come in useful for the next time that I drove there; and so that I wouldn't get hopelessly lost like we had done the year before. One country road in Somerset in the dark looks pretty much like another so that just a couple of miles from the motorway exit left me with not very much to go on. It would be down to Google Maps next time again.

A touch of nervous anticipation permeated throughout the coach and the laughter and general jollity seemed to diminish somewhat. I was not immune from this. Another point of no return. This was really, really it. I half-remembered that the roads were quite hilly the closer that you got to the festival site itself, and as the coach crested hill after hill, passing empty coaches coming away from the site in the opposite direction with "Glastonbury" as their destination, I knew that we were nearly there. One final hill and there it was; lying like a vast twinkling beautiful bedspread of lights in front of me. Seeing it from that view, the sheer size of the place was overwhelming, not just for me, but I think for everyone else on the coach. For a few seconds, not a sound could be heard apart from the noise of tyres on tarmac and the low, constant thrum of the engine. Jaws collectively dropped.

I looked at my watch (and this point, I do recall). 11.57. Just before midnight and the start of a new day. The coach seemed to take ages to get through the security gates and joined a long time of vehicles entering the site, all queued up and trying to get in. After 15 minutes or so of shenanigans we finally came to a halt behind some cowsheds in a large gravelled area. I was hoping that it wasn't too far away from the camping area, as I didn't fancy yomping for miles, with my heavy rucksack and the rest.

Before the coach could disgorge all its willing, yet slightly nervous volunteers, someone from Glastonbury hopped on to check all our credentials and give us our wristbands. One wristband was the usual Glasto fabric one; the other was some golden plastic one marked Avalon:Staff. This second one, we were told sagely, was to allow access to the campsite and all staff areas and was not to be lost under any circumstances. I proffered my wrist and I was tagged and ready to go.

Happily the to go bit was virtually a hop skip and a jump away from the coach; probably less than a couple of hundred meters away, so my back didn't have a chance to collapse with the weight of my rucksack. Someone in a hi-vis jacket directed me through a set of gate and there I was, actually back at Glastonbury, all set with tent in hand and looking forward to once again sleeping under the stars.

Chapter 5

The First Night

You'd think that the hard stuff was over by now and all I had to do was "pop-up" the "pop-up" tent and rest my weary head, but things are never that straightforward. Not where tents and me are concerned anyway.

When the coach had dropped everyone off and because of my general level of fitness i.e. close to zero, I was one of the last stragglers to actually get into the campsite. Which, because the coach from London had arrived some hours earlier, was already pretty full. Not to the same level as cheek-by-jowl camping on the main Glastonbury site but nevertheless, there weren't many options to choose from. A lot of tents were already up. As it was dark I didn't fancy negotiating my way past everyone who was already settled in while I was carrying all my stuff. I had imagined that the whole site would have all been floodlit so I could see what exactly needed to be done. However, it was if not totally pitch black, then fairly close to it. I found what I thought was a pretty much open space to put my tent up and got to work. (There was a reason why that gap was there which became very clear to me the next morning).

Despite my meticulous planning I hadn't packed the rucksack in the best way. I should have had everything I needed to pitch the tent at the top of the rucksack rather than buried between clothes and packets of biscuits. However, getting the tent itself up wasn't really an issue. Like the trial run, I unzipped the case and out it popped, hey presto! style. I looked like a pro. Until I had to rummaged through the rucksack for the guy ropes, mallet, tent pegs and oh shit, the ground sheet, which I really should have got out first. This I found sandwiched between t shirts and the airbed, again something that I should have packed near the top of the rucksack. I had therefore to move the erected but unsecured tent, a few feet out of the way to accommodate the ground sheet, then find the pegs to secure the ground sheet and then lift the tent back on top of the sheet. All this I was doing in the dark with my little torch clasped in my mouth.

Next to where I was going through this pantomime, three people were throwing up an immense tented structure with relative ease. Actually, it only seemed to be the work of one bloke; what I took for his better half and her mate were sipping glasses of wine and half-heartedly passing him ropes and poles when he called out for them. I took it that he must have been some ex-SAS/Ray Mears type because he had their tent up before I'd even managed to find my wonky mallet and bend the tent pegs into the ground. As for the guy ropes; well, I knew that they should be one double strand of tight cord but knots, string and my clumsy fingers have never seen eye-to-eye, and having to unravel a ball of nylon twine at nearly one o'clock in the morning, in the dark, in a field in Somerset, was never going to turn out too well. I got so pissed off with trying to untangle the thing that in the end one of the guy ropes was full of knots and at least four strands thick; it had no tension in it and was only there for effect. The other three guy ropes weren't even doubled over-although they were as tight as wire I doubted if they'd have been much use if the weather turned more than a bit breezy.

Although it was dark and I couldn't see much and didn't really know what I was doing, at least I could console myself with the fact that it wasn't raining and/or blowing a gale. Goodness knows how I would have coped if the weather was any way inclement. (Every year I have been to Glastonbury, the weather has been fine when I've been putting the tent up. Maybe I should really try for a proper trial run somewhere along the line and find a muddy field in the middle of February when the weather is especially bad. I'll do it in the middle of the night, with my wellies on the wrong feet and when I'm particularly tired. That should recreate the conditions that I surely will encounter one day if I keep on going to Glastonbury. If I could succeed it in that setting then I'd look as professional as everyone else).

The tent was then, if looking especially (or at all) like it should, at least standing upright-ish. Compared to my neighbours efforts it looked pitiful. Theirs was a tall structure with three separate rooms. All their guy ropes were perfectly positioned, fluorescent hi-viz things and the fabric of the tent was so taut then I'm sure that any rain would have just bounced off it. Mine looked like some ramshackle affair that had been abandoned after five days of hard living at Glastonbury and not just popped up mere minutes before. I wasn't optimistic about how it would turn out after a week. The final piece in the jigsaw was to blow up the airbed with the foot pump. It was well after one in the morning and by now I was completely knackered and more than a little pissed off. All I wanted to do was to lie down and sleep. It had been a long day. I do think that because I was so pissed off that I pumped the damn thing up so quickly. I vented my frustration through my feet and 10 minutes later I threw it into the tent and unravelled the sleeping bag on top of it.

My neighbours had asked me very kindly if I'd needed a hand but as I didn't want to appear inept so I had breezily declined their offers. In retrospect, it may have been a lot quicker if I had let them lend a hand. As I sat down for a smoke, they wandered over and offered me a drink. I don't normally drink brandy, but it went down a treat.

We exchanged a few pleasantries and had a bit of a chat, but by then I was so tired little was going in. What I did manage to take in was they'd worked Glasto the year before and that it was a quite good crack. I complemented them on their skills on putting up their tent and I suppose we must have spoken about the weather but ten minutes in and I was done for. Although they pressed me to have another drink and I was sorely tempted, tiredness had got the better of me. I crawled through the front of the tent, zipped it shut, wriggled into the sleeping bag and fell fast asleep. Tomorrow I'd wake up to see what exactly I'd let myself in for. My last thoughts were of endless motorways.

Chapter 6

On your marks

I'd had a bit of a fitful sleep, even though I was worn out from the travails of the day before. I felt around on the floor for my watch and saw it was only 6.30 a.m. I'd only had about 5 hours kip but I felt like I was raring to go. Maybe it was because I was sleeping on top of the air bed which I'd probably over inflated. This gave rise to the feeling of lying on top of an extremely bouncy trampoline rather than a soft, supportive, all-enveloping fluffy cloud. At any moment it felt as if the airbed would decide to throw me off of its own volition. A few days however, with my not insubstantial frame lying on top of it would, no doubt cause some loss of air and therefore an increase in comfort. More pressing on my mind was the fact that I needed to empty my bladder and didn't really know where I'd pitched my tent in relation to the toilets. I wasn't looking forward to a long hike.

Unzipping the tent, I poked my head out and scanned the scene. Luckily (in one sense) I didn't have to walk very far. I had pitched my tent up about 15 yards from the portaloos and the showers. In fact no-one else had put their tents up so close to these very handy facilities. In the darkness of the previous night, I hadn't cottoned onto the reason why there was a spare patch of ground for my tent was precisely because it was so close to the toilets. That was a bit daft of me to say the least. Furthermore, and more significantly as it turned out (though I didn't realise it that morning), was that my tent was pitched right at the only entrance to the camping area. This meant that everyone who wanted to get to their tent had to pass mine. And my tent seemed to bisect the main route onto the site, everyone would either have to walk on the left or right side of my tent. It was if my little two-man tent was a mini roundabout that had been placed at the most inconvenient point in the road. At this juncture, I was more concerned that I was so close to the portaloos, but over time that was the least of my concerns.

I inelegantly popped out of the tent; there really is no other way, not that I can see anyway. It is seemingly impossible to look in any sense graceful. Thankfully there weren't many people around and I sauntered down the 15 yards or so to the toilets in relative isolation. Scanning the sky, there wasn't a patch of blue to be seen; it was uniformly grey and cloudy. It didn't auger, but I was in need of a coffee and the mess tent was right in front of me. I knew that there would be an upside of pitching the tent where I did.

One of the things we had been given on the coach with the wristbands were meal vouchers; three meals vouchers for each day we were working i.e. breakfast, dinner and tea. Additionally we were all informed that tea and coffees were free and unlimited. This was more than fine with me. First things first. I saw a big water urn at the end of the tent and made myself a coffee. Looking around, the tent was a big canvas structure, with enough trestle tables to seat a couple of hundred people. At one end was a serving counter, with hot and cold plates and behind that, covered with a canvas curtain was clearly a large kitchen. At this stage there were only maybe have a dozen souls scattered at random at the tables. They all seemed fairly half-asleep and I needed to have at least one coffee and a ciggie before I was up to anything resembling a conversation. I took my coffee outside and sat by the door of the tent. I made a brief phone call home to update everyone with how things were and to see what the BBC were saying about the weather. "Possible light showers and cloudy" seemed to be the order of the day, but I think I could have guessed as much by casting my eyes heavenwards.

First coffee and cigarette of the day dutifully despatched it was time to sample the fare from inside. I wasn't wholly optimistic regarding what it would be like, but it all came as a pleasant surprise. (And with running the risk of making this sound like some sort of Little Chef promo there was a choice of cereals, white or brown toast, jam, marmalade and/or full cooked English (sausages, eggs, bacon, beans, fried bread, mushrooms, beans etc. Makes me quite peckish just typing it. And it does sound like it should be printed and laminated). Knowing I would possibly have a full day ahead of me, I plumped (an appropriate word) for the full English. And the toast. With a bowl of cornflakes as a little starter.

By the time all that had been seen off-as well as a post-breakfast coffee and ciggie, the tent was getting quite full and everyone was getting set for the 10.00 a.m. briefing. This does sound as if it was some quasi-military operation and in many ways I guess it was. I wouldn't have fancied being the person responsible for pulling the assembled motley crew together however. The vast majority of them seemed to be groups of student-aged students (clearly) who'd seemed to congregate in clumps of half a dozen or so, all talking over each other and making quite a racket. There were a much smaller number of older couples and the like (all in their mid-thirties or so), who looked as if they had done this before. They had a battle-weary jaded air and seemed very au fait with the set up. The smallest group (which I seemed to one of) were-to stretch the military analogy- older than everyone else there and by-and-large were by themselves, looking like older conscripts in a Home Guard sort of bewildered way. The expressions on the faces of these befuddled gentlefolk (myself included) was a sort of "How did we get here? Are you sure we are supposed to be here? What are we here for?"

In any event, trying to marshal all these disparate groups together would not be an easy task and would have needed someone who "would not have any messing around". Fortunately, Avalon had exactly the right person to take charge. Up stepped a formidable woman. She was, I guess, in her mid-fifties and was wearing a well-worn Barbour jacket (clearly not for show) and a pair of glasses on her head and another pair around her neck. Her hair was all over the place and in general, the level of dishellevement gave the appearance that she'd been dragged through one of the hedges at Glastonbury both backwards and forwards. This all belied a steely core that became clear as soon as she opened her mouth. This was not someone who needed a megaphone.

"Morning everyone," she announced, "Could I please ask you to pay attention for a few minutes as there are some things I need to run through?"

This was quite clearly an instruction, a command rather than a request.

"I said, "Good morning"".

That got the whole attention of the tent quite quickly and she managed to get over 500 people to stop talking, laughing and eating in the blink of an eye. Once everyone's eyes were on her, she carried on.

"My name is Shirley and I'm the Avalon Manager whilst you are here. If you have any issues or problems or anything you need to check then you can see me or any of my team."

There were a group of people standing next to her all holding clipboards and walkie- talkies, looking very loyal and ready to do her bidding.

"We are in the caravan right next to this tent. I'm going to run through a few things that you need to know but I promise I'll try to be quick."

At this point she smiled, and I understood that she wasn't all that bad. Probably the right sort of person that you could rely upon if needed. She then rapidly explained how things were going to work. We would all be sent with the various bar managers shortly with specific bars we'd been assigned to. There we'd be given some training and familiarisation ready for us to start working. The bar managers were very experienced, she said, and they were the people we could turn to should we have any problems on the ground. The other points she stressed were that we could not under any circumstances, serve drinks to anyone who was under age, or in our eyes looked under age. This would lead to the individual volunteer being thrown out of Glastonbury there and then, without a second chance and possibly with the bar being closed down. Furthermore, if we didn't turn up for a shift or if we turned up late or pissed that would be it as well. Goodbye festival. This was fair enough to me, but as the festival went on it was clear that a few people thought that they could either get away with it or just didn't listen (or care) as tales of miscreants being escorted off by security were manifold.

The only thing that surprised me really was that she kept going on about Shelter volunteers and didn't mention anything about EJF. I thought this was a bit odd, but as they'd let me and everyone else on the bus from Sheffield onto the site, then I wasn't going to argue the point. There was clearly a literal bus-load of EJF volunteers alongside me so I wasn't in the wrong place.

"You should all know what groups and bars you've been assigned to," announced Shirley. "As I call out each group then could you all join up with your bar managers and head off to your bars?" She shouted the letters A and then B. A general melee ensued, and by the time she'd got to the letter H the whole tent was a scene of noise, chaos and confusion with people trying to find their respective groups. Cups of tea and coffee were knocked to the ground and it looked like the most disorganised scene possible. It was hard to imagine these people being able to serve a pint if they couldn't get this sorted out. I stood on the edge of this madness and waited for it all to subside. I glanced across at Shirley and her team. She displayed an air of bemusement and obviously had gone through this before; she wasn't rushing into action and after five minutes or so everything had settled down.

It was at this point that I joined up with my group; which appeared to contain nobody who was on the bus with me from Sheffield. Demographically, they seemed to be made up pretty much as the whole set up as before; mostly students, a few older-ish couples (including my neighbours who I'd spoken with the night before) and another couple of older people like myself. There were about 30 of us in total. The bar managers; four of them, two blokes and two women, gathered us altogether and told us to follow them to the bar where we'd run through everything.

During the time we'd been in the tent it had started drizzling. Not heavy rain, but a constant drizzle that kept up all day. I had taken the precaution of putting on my wellies that morning and that was a good decision as the ground was getting softer and softer underfoot. These wellies remained on my feet for days and by the end of the festival I came to hate them with a vengeance. I think that if I'd worn them for much longer then, as a process of evolution, my feet would have turned into a pair of rubberised appendages.

One of the bar managers, Phil, a chap in his late twenties/early thirties I guessed, told us that it was a bit of a walk to the bar and we might like to take a bottle of water with us. I didn't like the sound of this "bit of a walk" thing, but being a tough Northern bloke (unlike the Southern softies) didn't go for the bottle of water option, and preferred another coffee and lit up a ciggie to help me on my way.

It was indeed, a bit of a trek to the bar and took about half an hour. The campsite itself was just outside of the main site on the other side of the tall metal fence that runs around the festival like a steel ring. We had therefore to go through the entrance gate, all of us getting our two wristbands checked before we were let in. The campsite was on the west side of the site (I think, although geography has never been a strong point with me), and the "Music and Cider" bar where I would be working, was between the Pyramid and Other Stage i.e. pretty much in the middle of the whole thing.

Like a school trip we walked crocodile style through the gates, along a service road at the top of the hill and dropped down past the Pyramid and through the now increasingly soggy grass towards the Other Stage. This half-hour walk gave me a chance to get to know who I would possibly be working with. Most of them seemed to have been recruited through Shelter and not EJF and for most of them it was their first time working a bar, so in that sense I was a step ahead. (Possibly not that far ahead as I'd forgotten really everything I learnt about bar work. A bit like O-level French). Most of them; probably all of them, were younger than me, so I did feel like the tag-along, B & Q token old person. Most of them seemed to be from London and/or the South; there didn't seem to be anyone from Liverpool, or indeed anywhere in the North West. I think I heard a Yorkshire accent drifting from the back, but they have a tendency to do that anyway. It may have been just blown on the wind from an adjacent field.

As we reached the bar, I remembered it from the previous year; or at least its location. Then, it was kitted out to resemble a garden in a country pub; this year it had a very faint quasi-Hawaiian theme. No doubt they had paid a fortune for some young design graduate to come up with something novel, but it all looked a bit tatty and cheap. It was how you would imagine a film set to look like. All MDF and fake brickwork. It looked as if a slight gust of wind would cause it to fall over.

Something in common with my tent. I wasn't bothered though about what it was made from, this is for mere description. I was more concerned about what exactly I had to do.

We all stood around for a bit while Phil and the other bar managers had a bit of a conflab. They came back with the news that the bar wasn't quite finished i.e. there was no power for the next 30 minutes or so and we couldn't really be shown anything. Furthermore, because the sparks were still working on it, we couldn't enter the bar yet; but there was no point in trekking back so could we just hang around for a bit? There was no point as far as I could see in wandering around in the drizzle for half-an-hour; many (if not most) of the stalls nearby weren't set up yet or open and most of the group seemed to think the same way, so we stood around and chatted about inconsequential stuff for that time.

When the green light was given we were split up into groups of a dozen or so; these were the teams we would be working with on our shifts. This is when our intensive training started. Phil led us behind the bar to show us the ropes. There were two sides to the bar. The first ran parallel to the pathway to the Other Stage i.e. it faced outwards and the second side ran parallel (or backwards) to that and faced a covered area about 50 square foot in total. This covered area had a solid-ish flat roof and walls made of plywood rather than canvas. There wasn't anything different about the floor; it was just the bare ground. A few roughly hewn wooden benches, painted in primary colours were scatttered around at random. Because the main colour for the walls and ceiling (and really everything else apart from the benches) was a muddy looking brown, it all appeared a tad gloomy. There was a raised stage at one end, with a P.A. and lighting rig all in place. I supposed that this was the music element of the music and cider bar.

As for the cider element of the bar, well that was it. All the bar would be selling was cider. Nothing else but cider. No lager, no spirits, no wine, no soft drinks. Nothing that I hadn't heard of before. All my extensive (yet fruitless) research of Thomas and Amy to discover exactly what the kids were drinking had been a waste of time. Not only was the bar only selling cider, it wasn't as if there were lots of different brands or even many different types that could cause confusion. It was like the Model T Ford of bars. You could have anything to drink as long as it was Gaymers Apple Cider. Or Gaymers Pear Cider. (As I discovered later, and not unsurprisingly, this limited choice didn't stop punters prevaricating between the two). The only other choice was that you could buy them in halves or in pints. This wasn't especially difficult as there were no half-pint glasses; you just had to serve the pint glasses half full. So that was four possible combinations; apple or pear; pints or halves. And when I say glasses, as glass isn't allowed at Glastonbury, that meant paper cups.

There were no pumps as I recognised them at the bar. There were, but these weren't connected to anything and were only for show. Instead, in the middle of the bar; between the two bars, there were two large square stainless steel contraptions. Phil explained that these machines delivered the cider and one was for the apple; the other was for the pear. There were twelve nozzles to each machine, in an array of 4 x 3 and this would deliver a dozen pints at a time. For pints you pressed a button twice, and for halves once. The halves looked a bit forlorn when poured into a pint size cup, but I don't think that it was anticipated that many halves would be sold anyway.

After this we moved onto the complexities of tills and pricing. And this was how it was. Pints were £4.20 and halves were, well, £2.10. The tills were normal tills with normal buttons but virtually all of them were irrelevant. They'd been set up so there was no need to key in £4.20 (or multiples of £.4.20).To enter a pint you had to type in "1" and for a half it was "2". For multiples all you had to do was either press the button more than once, or if you got really adept, you could use the multiplication sign. Additionally, there were also laminated sheets either side of the till showing how much one to ten pints would cost; but by the end of my 3 shifts I was able to recite the 42 times table in my sleep. I could also work in the 21 times table as and when required.

That was it really; Phil showed us where the paper cups were kept (in boxes under the bar) and where we could make a brew during our breaks and we were virtually done. This had taken all of 15 minutes and made me feel a bit daft about getting so stressed out about it all beforehand. This would be a piece of piss. (Something that I will now forever associate very strongly with cider in paper cups). He then gathered us all round and gave us a final message about not serving drinks to anyone under age at all and to check i/d if we were in anyway uncertain. There was another bit about turning up on time for our shifts (and that it would probably take us longer to get there when the festival was fuller than it had that morning). The killer point was something I'd always craved for but never realised it save in a subconscious sense; the chance to wear a t-shirt with the word "crew" on it. (How childish! And at 51 years old as well!). Every time we did a shift we'd have to wear a red (no other colour available, but as a Liverpool FC fan I could live with that; at least it wasn't blue), with Shelter's name and logo on the front and the word "crew" on the back. I know it wasn't as if I had an access-all-areas laminated pass so I could hob-nob backstage at the Pyramid with Beyonce, Bono and Chris Martin, yet it was as close as I was ever going to get. (All things are not as they seem however, and there'll be a bit more about the crew t-shirts in a bit).

But that was all it done. Nothing really planned for a full day or so which gave me a chance to wander round (in the rain) a bit. Whilst we'd been waiting for the training to start, I'd had a chat with one of the security guards. (That's what's good about Glastonbury, amongst many other things. There is always someone around who wants to chat, or is willing to chat or just share the whole thing). He told me that there were already over 80,000 people on site even by Wednesday afternoon and that it was filling up very quickly. At least I wasn't one of those wandering around like a lost soul and trying to find a spare patch of ground to pitch the tent.

I was intending to potter around for a bit, (that's what's good about being over 50 years old-I have the ability to potter; something that is impossible to do if I was much younger). I wanted to see how things were getting on, but I thought it would be a good idea to check on the tent and see how it was holding up against the rain. Admittedly, it wasn't some intense storm with heavy rain and driving winds; it wasn't even raining constantly. It was more of one of those summer showers;

light drizzle every now and then. Weak, watery sun trying to break through the clouds.

I trudged back towards the campsite. It had been a good decision to wear my wellies as my feet were sinking into the soft grass more and more. Patches of mud and small puddles were already forming where the ground dipped and wherever there had been lots of people walking. As I walked along the metal tracks and towards the Pyramid, it all seemed very strange compared to the previous year. We'd only turned up on the Thursday afternoon in 2010 and had a nightmare finding anywhere at all to put our tent up. This time, a day earlier, I was walking in the opposite direction to the vast majority of people who were struggling along with unpacked tents and heavy rucksacks. I felt a bit guilty about feeling a certain amount of smug self-satisfaction that my tent was already up and that I was heading back to somewhere where I could get hot food and free coffee, as well as hot showers on demand. This was tempered by the thought that it was quite likely or at least fairly possible that my tent skills were at a level where the slightest amount of precipitation would have resulted in a camping disaster. As I stood by the Pyramid Stage, having a coffee and a ciggie, watching everything being put into place, I had visions, if not of everything being washed away (it hadn't been raining *that* hard), then maybe that my packet of custard creams could have got a bit soggy. This is the extent of my rock and roll lifestyle. Potentially soggy biscuits. This caused me to hot foot it back to the tent sooner than I had planned. It's difficult to hot foot it anywhere while wearing a pair of wellies, so I just walked back a touch more quickly.

On the way down to the bar I hadn't fully appreciated that we had been walking down hill most of the way; probably because I was chatting all the way to my future co-workers and taking in all the sights. On the way back, by myself however, I slowly understood that to get back to the campsite that whichever way I went, it meant navigating a few hills; either a short, but very steep one at the back of the Pyramid, or a longer, but not as steep a hike through a different exit gate and then skirting around the fence. Whichever way I decided, it was largely uphill and it all took the wind out my sails a bit about having everything set up.

It took me just over 40 minutes to saunter, as quickly as I could, back to the campsite. This gave me a general indication of how long it would take in future. (Or so I thought). All the way back, I kept thinking of the things I'd done with Amy the previous year and the places at Glasto we'd seen and been to. I half-expected to look around and find her next to me, rabbitting away, twenty to the dozen. But she wasn't, however much I wanted her to be. I wanted to turn around and say, "Look at that, remember being there last time?" It was certainly going to be different this year.

I wasn't going to get too maudlin however. It had been so difficult and long-winded in just getting to Glastonbury that I was determined to enjoy it. As I got back to the campsite, and before I plucked up courage to check on the tent, I thought that I should make a quick call home. (Other people would, and do, and were, texting furiously. Texting and I do not get on well. Maybe it's because of my phone (being old, used and unloved) or maybe it's just some inherent luddite tendency of mine, but I wasn't going to start all this "How R U? I am OK.CU L8r" nonsense. It was easier just to press the phone button and speak. Even that isn't easy for me. I have, on many occasions, cut conversations half-way through, totally by accident, because I don't really know what I'm doing). On this occasion though I actually managed to switch the phone on and get through straight away. As Amy was in work, I couldn't speak with her and tell her how things were, but Jackie had everything at her fingertips. I felt like an astronaut at the space station and Jackie was the control centre. In Liverpool as opposed to Houston of course, yet she had all bases covered.

"How's things? Did you get there ok? Is the tent alright?" (I swear I heard muffled giggles at that point).

After updating her quickly (I didn't want to run the battery on the phone down too quickly) on everything that had happened-the journey, the tent, the food and the bar, everyone I was working with, what shifts I would be working etc, I came to the most pressing question of all. "What's the weather forecast like? What does the BBC say?"

She is a marvel. If it had been the other way round I would have been unprepared for that and would have spent precious time getting it up on the internet. Jackie however, had the page open on the browser as we spoke.

"Cloudy but dry later today. Bit of rain of Friday but warm. Saturday the same. Sunday fine all day. That sounds ok, doesn't it? Only a bit of rain."

Only a bit of rain. That could mean anything in relation to the tent, but I wasn't going to admit over the phone that I wasn't optimistic about it holding up to the rigorous of a bit of light drizzle. I didn't want Jackie worrying unnecessarily and I certainly wasn't going to admit that the tent looked a bit, well, haphazard.

"That sounds ok, bit of rain is just a bit of rain. It's been drizzling a bit this today but it's stopped now. I'm just having a coffee and a ciggie and sitting by the mess tent. How's Amy and Thomas? Any other news?"

Everyone was fine and there was no other news. (Like going on holiday for a couple of weeks, I always expect things to have changed radically back home, but they never do). Jackie told me the latest news from the BBC about Glasto; about how many people were there already and that the photos on the Glasto website of everyone arriving looked fantastic. And that was it really. She told me to save the battery on the phone and I said I'd call her later. I was getting rather peckish and it was well after time to get something to eat. Having something to eat would give me an excuse not to check the tent and to buy a bit of time. Delaying the inevitable. On the other hand, if I craned my neck and peered over from the front of the mess tent where I was sitting, I could easily see my tent as I'd pitched it so close. It looked ok, from what I could see, but maybe I should really go over and make sure. It was only about 15 yards away.

Surprisingly, it was perfectly fine. Nothing had leaked and even my custard creams were intact and as dry as a biscuit (isn't that the correct term?). I think that this was largely due more to the hydrostatic properties of the tent itself, rather than my abilities. The guy ropes had held up as well, but as there wasn't a breath of wind, I don't think that they had been overworked. All was well with the world. I glanced at my watch. The day had flown by; it was nearly half past four and no wonder I was ready for something to eat. Maybe I had sauntered too much on the way back from the bar; maybe I had lingered too long watching the Pyramid being put together; maybe I'd spent too long making notes and people watching. That's the effect Glastonbury has at times. Without going too hippy-ish, time can sometimes become at bit nebulous at Glastonbury. Whether that's because of some mystic ley-line type thing or just that you're not in the day-to- day routine I'm not entirely sure. Well, I am actually. It's because you're not tied up with the usual humdrum nature of work and the like. Nothing to do with ley-lines, crystals or any other such rubbish. But I was having to take due notice of the time this year, so I had to make sure that my watch was ok and that it all didn't become somewhat arbitrary and irrelevant. I didn't want to commit the ultimate faux-pas and turn up late for a shift. And while that massive breakfast had stood by me well, it was time to get something to eat.

A big plate comprising chicken pie, chips and beans did the trick. Bread and butter helped a bit as well. A follow up of sponge pudding and custard together with a cup of tea rounded things off a treat. I don't want to get too Proustian at this point, but every time I've had chicken pie since, it has taken me back to that Wednesday afternoon in that mess tent at Glastonbury. I feel my shoes on the floor and expect to have the soft feel of grass rather than solid floor and look up and expect to see walls made of white canvas than wall paper. Maybe a chicken pie is North West England's equivalent to a Parisian Madeline.

It had taken me some time to finish this meal and whilst I had intended to go on another wander that evening, I was in two minds about wandering around the whole site, fairly aimlessly for a couple of hours at a time when it appeared that a lot of things were still being set up. Having said that, it would have been of interest and I was curious to see what was different and what I might discover.

My plans to go a-wandering (with my knapsack on my back) were curtailed -out of choice- as I ended in up in conversation with a few people in the tent. I got chatting with a bloke sitting next to me, who like me, had got the gig because he couldn't get tickets and had been to Glasto a fair few times in the past. Kevin was in his early forties and from somewhere like Kent (or somewhere "down South"; my grasp of geography and recollection isn't that complete. I feel a bit guilty about this. I can't really criticise anyone else for lumping everyone north of Birmingham as "Northerner", yet can't distinguish myself between someone who lives in Kent and someone who's from say, Devon).

By the time we had discussed how we'd ended up working at Glasto, what bars we would be working (Kevin was assigned to a bar near West Holts and therefore expected it to be quite busy),what work we did back home, music, families, kids and all matter of things it had turned dusk and then dark. It seemed somewhat daft to wander around the site; it would have taken an hour just to walk anywhere and walk back and I decided to call it a day. It seemed a long time since I struggled out of the tent that morning and I was tired. I made a quick call home to say goodnight and headed back to the tent. Tomorrow would be the first working day and I needed to get a good nights' kip.

Chapter 7

Now the real work starts

The plan had been to get a good nights' sleep. That had been the plan. I had travelled to Glasto with a bit of a cold (not strictly man-flu, but a cold nevertheless). It wasn't really a cold either, more of a sniffle and a bit of a cough. It did mean that I probably only slept for a couple of hours at a time. Maybe my broken sleep was due in part to thinking what would be facing me on my first day back behind a bar, though I can't be sure of that. I remember looking at my watch and seeing it was about 6.15 a.m. It was already light outside and I lay in the tent, staring at the walls of the tent, which were wet with condensation, until 7 -ish before making a move.

Of course the first thing I had to do was get a coffee from the mess tent. There were a few souls around, but it was generally deserted. I sat outside the tent sipping the coffee and had a smoke. That brought me back to life somewhat and whilst the shower block was fairly empty, I thought it would be a good idea to give it a go before having any breakfast.

It would be fair to say that compared to the washing facilities on the rest of the site for the ordinary punters that working three 8 hours shifts was worth it just to be able to have a hot shower and a shave. These showers were truly magnificent and a revelation. Unlike the few showers on the main site, which seemed to me to be both a) fairly rudimentary and b) always busy with long queues, and therefore not really worth going for on either counts, these ones were a much more sophisticated set up. There were two shower blocks; each of which had four showers and each block was the size of a large static caravan. I think that they were built upon a caravan chassis or converted caravans anyway; they were on wheels and were a few feet from the ground. This doesn't sound very promising and not in any manner what would be needed. However, on opening the door to each shower, you were faced with a fully tiled shower cubicle, a separate sink and a mirror on the wall. The showers were available 24 hours a day and were fully plumbed in. I turned the shower on and expected a bit of a dribble of tepid water but what came out was a powerful jet of hot water. This would do for me! I am not overstating things too much to say that this was a few hundred quid in itself or the price of working a few nights. It certainly beat just having baby wipe washes for 6 consecutive days.

The only difficulty, post-shower wise I found was being able to get your wellies back on again without getting covered in mud, but after a few days I managed to work out a strategy which although not very elegant, seemed to suffice. It involved balancing on one leg, making sure that your clean-socked foot didn't touch the muddy ground whilst you whipped a welly on the other foot. Not very rock and roll-I bet that Bono and the rest at the Pyramid didn't have such issues; they probably had welly roadies.

Suitably refreshed after the power shower, it was time for breakfast. By now the mess tent had filled up considerably compared to what it was like at 7.00 a.m. and I had to queue a while for my full English. There weren't many unoccupied seats either, which as it turned out was a good thing. I ended sitting next to my next-door neighbours. To my embarrassment, I had forgotten their names although they remembered mine, even though they had introduced themselves to me on the Tuesday night. (I do have this issue at times, when I just don't register someone's name, even though it may only be minutes after I've been told what it is. I don't think it's my age as I always have been like that. I guess that it will only get worse as I get older). I had to work through a process of elimination, over a 45 minute conversation, to discover that they were Rob, Julie and Becky and that Rob and Julie were married; and that Becky was Julie's best friend. That cleared all that up then.

They had worked Glastonbury bars for the past three years and wouldn't do it any other way. They also knew all of the bar managers that were working in the Cider bar and therefore were able to give me some useful tips. Their general consensus was that Phil and John, were both ok and were generally quite fair and that Karen, the third manager, was a good laugh and "very nice". On the other hand, they all warned me about Sue.

"She is a real bitch," said Julie, "Just watch your back."

I raised a quizzical eyebrow, just to gain more information. Rob nodded. "She's really lazy herself and won't lift a finger, but God help you if you put a foot wrong, she'll be on you like a ton of bricks."

"Really?" I said.

"Absolutely," he explained, "She was there last year and we couldn't believe it when we saw her again. We can't believe that they've still employed her."

To complete this picture, Becky waded in. "She got someone kicked out last year because she said that they weren't pulling their weight and not up to it, not because they'd served someone under-age or not turned up, but just because she didn't like them. It was her word against theirs and she won."

"And she made sure that everyone knew it was down to her as well," said Julie.

"We sent really negative feedback to Avalon about her afterwards," said Rob, "Anonymously, because we wanted to make sure we were ok for this year, of course, but it doesn't seem to have made any difference." They all shook their heads. "We were just so surprised to see her again. I mean, she *seems* very nice and smiley, but as soon as your back is turned she'll be bitching about you to the other managers."

"And to the rest of the crew as well," said Becky "She's just so...unprofessional."

"Well, my first shift is this morning," I said, "I'd better be careful!" They all wished me luck and with their words of warning echoing in my ears, I promised to report back to them later. Rob said that they might pop by during the afternoon to see how I was getting on and to offer some moral support-although they were working the Cider bar as well, none of our shifts coincided and in fact, they weren't starting until Friday. I left them to finish off their breakfasts and nipped back to the tent (just to make sure it was all secure for the rest of the day) with a coffee before heading off to the bar. I didn't want to be late on my first day and get into trouble with Bitchy Karen.

I took all the words of warning with a pinch of salt, to be honest. It could have all been a bit of a personality clash; Rob, Julie and Becky appeared a tad, well, self-assured themselves and I wasn't going to take their judgement of the said Karen purely on face value. But it was good to know what I was potentially wading in to, and forewarned is forearmed and all such similar clichés sprung to mind.

Getting into the site through the entrance gates was straightforward. Although there were long-ish queues for the public to get in, I was able to go through the staff gate with relative ease. "Relative ease" counted as walking up to the staff and crew entrance, having my wristbands checked and walking onto the site. This was easier than spending ages waiting in line behind late comers to the festival, complete with assorted bags, tents, prams, trolleys, gazebos, wheelbarrows and all things essential, inessential, irrelevant and ridiculous.

I still had an hour or so before I had to get to the bar and start my shift. This gave me time to have a coffee and make a quick call home. Jackie told me that the weather forecast was much the same as it had been the previous day and that there should be no rain all day, although it would be cloudy. The little bit of rain during Wednesday, combined with thousands of people arriving on site and stomping over already soft ground had caused every single pathway to turn into gloopy, sticky mud. Where there were any blades of grass left standing, these quickly disappeared as soon as they came into contact with the gentlest footfall. The mud, at this early stage was just about navigable and not at the stage where every step felt as if may end in disaster. It was as if you were walking across a muddy field. Actually, it was walking across a muddy field. Just an inconvenience at this point. (It was soon to turn into something much, much worse. But on that Thursday morning I managed to get to the bar in about 45 minutes; the mud didn't hold me up that much, it was more to do with getting past the hordes of festival goers; some desperately still trying to find somewhere to pitch their tents and others already pissed beyond comprehension. Most people however were just heading in the opposite direction to which I was going.

As I got closer and closer to the bar, I felt strangely as if I was an 11 year-old on my first day at big school. After all, for the past 25 years I had worked in the relative security of the Civil Service. Cocooned, if you want to put it that way. And here I was going out into the big bad wide world again, where there were no clear lines of management and mentoring; no welfare officers or HR departments; no interim reviews or annual reports; no tea clubs or any of that cosiness. It seemed so much like moving from Junior School to big school where you were at the bottom of the pecking order and the big bad lads would stuff you into dustbins on your first day or even worse (of course, these things never happen to anyone at big school, but these urban myths seem to continue, generation after generation). Lest anyone who has never worked for the Civil Service thinks that it is all any easy ride, where we have gold-plated pensions, sit around drinking tea all day, have unlimited annual leave and just basically take the piss; well, I may have given the wrong impression. It's not like that at all. But having worked in the past outside of the Civil Service, I do know that it is different and a lot more cut throat out in the "real world".

As I walked (or rather, squelched) down towards the Pyramid stage it did cross my mind that if I fucked it up, either through ignorance or sheer incompetence, then all of this could be over before it really started.

But I did have a few positive things in my favour however and as I got nearer to the bar, my plan of winging it all was fully formed and set in my mind. (As much as any plan based on "winging it" can be). The three things that I knew I could rely upon- apart from my ready wit, sheer cunning and stunningly good looks for a 51 year old-were the following; firstly, I had worked a bar before (and busy ones at that), so I knew I could do it. Secondly, I reckoned I was fairly competent at my day job and that a quarter of a century's experience working as a manager and dealing with many different types of people surely had to count for something. Additionally, I did have age on my side. I wasn't going to be phased by working with a bunch of kids who were as young, if not younger than my own children. It was all just a matter of working these three shifts, keeping my head down and having a bit of a laugh. At least it should provide valuable writing material. I'd just grit my teeth and deal with Bitchy Karen if, as and when it all arose.

I'd timed it just right as I got to the bar with about 15 minutes to spare. Phil beckoned me to go through the door at the back where there were already a couple of the team waiting.

"Morning!" he announced to everyone, quite breezily. "Hope you are all set for a busy day?" I took it that he was being slightly ironic at this juncture as there didn't seem to be massed hordes queuing up waiting for the bar to open. (Unlike the Weatherspoons by home, but that's another story-and culture, altogther).

"Right," he said, "Only a few things to mention before it all kicks off. You'll need to get one of the crew t-shirts. They are all over there."

He pointed to what I'd assumed were cardboard boxes of rubbish waiting to be thrown out. It looked like a collection of rags, all jumbled up. In fact the whole back area of the bar was a bit ramshackle. There were a couple of trestle tables, a safe, a kettle, (with an assortment of various mugs lying around), generators, cabling and other mysterious technology. It all gave the general impression that the bar had been up and running for weeks, as opposed to only one or two shifts. It didn't auger well for the rest of the weekend.

"Don't forget to ask for i/d if you are anyway unsure. Me and John will be here all day, so if there is anything you need then please ask us. Everyone will have a half hour break through the shifts but we'll work that out, depending on how busy it is. Oh, and make yourselves a cup of tea before you start if you'd like."

I thought that I'd better get hold of a t-shirt while I could and before all the larger sizes went. (Mind you, as most of the team appeared as if they could do with a good pan of scouse, I didn't think that this would be a problem). There was a problem however, and it specifically related to me.

Although I was looking forward to the somewhat dubious kudos of being able to wear an item of clothing with the word "crew" emblazoned on it, I hadn't factored in that these shirts wouldn't exactly be bespoke fashion items and that Avalon clearly weren't going to spend a fortune on these. In fact, I think that they had spent as little as possible. I am not averse at all to spending as little as possible of clothes- I am at a stage where comfort and price come way ahead of fashion and style every time-but I know that the shirts were made from the cheapest material that could be found. That didn't bother me at all. The issue was that Avalon, in a clear attempt to keep costs to a minimum, had seemingly only ordered 3 different sizes of shirts; small, medium and large. With the best will in the world, a medium was never going to do for me, and large, well, size is all relative and it's been a good few years since large ever entered my head as a size appropriate for me. (I do think that sizes of shirts have gone the way of sliced bread. I mean, you can't get hold of thin sliced bread anymore. What was thin sliced 20 years ago, is now at best, medium and sometimes, thick. I'll buy a thick sliced loaf, get it home and think, "Thick? Are you kidding me? If this is thick then goodness knows how thin medium will be."). All this is a (none-too) subtle way of pointing out that I ended up in a bit of a frantic attempt in searching the bottom of the cardboard box in vain for an xl shirt but there were none to be found. I didn't want to appear too desperate so I grabbed what I hoped was one of the largest looking large ones and went for that. It was always going to be touch and go as to whether I could actually get it on but due to the cheapness of the fabric it seemed to have a bit of inbuilt stretch and this worked in my favour. I pulled the damn thing over my head and it fitted like a glove. An extremely tight glove, but it fitted. Everywhere. I was scared of breathing too hard in case it ripped every seam in an Incredible Hulk style. At least it would keep me warm if it got a bit chilly, but my dreams of appearing cool whilst wearing a "crew" shirt had evaporated very quickly. All this messing around with the shirt left me with no time for a cup of tea before the shift started; it was now 10.58 and time to stop messing around. This was it.

I'd like to be able to give a second-by-second account of my first shift, but all I have are impressions and stray memories; it wasn't as if it was so busy that I couldn't makes notes. It was more monotonous than anything else. It was really like riding a bike; the moment that I stepped behind the bar, I was hit with a big sense of déjà-vu. I'd worked mad busy bars before so this wouldn't be a problem. There was a constant thought in the back of my mind that in eight hours it would be over and I would therefore be a third of the way through my commitment.

As the first punter turned up for their first drink (of many, no doubt), the only question I had to ask them was if they wanted apple or pear cider. It was as easy as that and after a little while I realised that no-one was going to mess around with halves; it was a safe assumption to work on the premise that pints were the order of the day. I can't honestly recall if it was particularly busy or not. I don't think it was because my notes made after the other shifts used the words "crazy" and frenetic" and such terms weren't touched upon on the Thursday. After all this time, I don't have a firm grasp on what happened during those 8 hours. This is odd because I can remember in fairly precise detail all the lead up to it and what happened afterwards. Maybe it was because it was either so inherently boring or that it was something psychologically I've blocked out. The latter sounds a bit too dramatic and therefore I think that the boring option is the one to go for.

What I do know is that once I'd served my first pint, used the till for the first time and worked out how to multiply £4.20 any number of times to any sensible level, really that was it. Half an hour in and I was counting the hours down. I'd got chatting to the rest of the team in brief, snatched conversations and by and large, they seemed ok. Apart from me, there were a couple of "older" folk; Steve, from Exeter was about 40-ish and there was Lynn from somewhere indistinct in the Midlands who was also in the same age bracket. No-one as old as I was however. For both Steve and Lynn it was their first Glastonbury and they both seemed to have stumbled into the job on a bit of a whim. For both of them a major driver was being able to do the festival at a minimal cost and although the tickets themselves are only £200 once you add the cost of transport, getting all the gear together and some cash for food and drinks that figure could easily be doubled or trebled quite quickly. Before you know it, a few days at Glastonbury would add up to a tidy sum and at least the cost of a cheap foreign holiday. Now cheap holidays in the sun aren't everyone's idea of fun, but as we surveyed the darkening skies and increasingly muddy vistas from our side of the bar, there was something appealing about five days in Benidorm as opposed to five days in Somerset.

Both Steve and Lynn had travelled by themselves and it was quite odd that although all three of us worked the same shifts we never bumped into one another anywhere else; apart from the campsite or the mess tent, we never saw each other anywhere else at the festival. Maybe it wasn't that odd though; Lynn (very nice person, but a bit quiet) was a bit of an unreconstructed hippy and spent a lot of her time at the festival in the Healing Fields and all that stuff. Steve, on the other hand, was a pipe-smoking, bearded, real ale aficionado who intended to see many of the acts playing in the acoustic tent. Not exactly my cup of Earl Grey, but I suppose out of all the team we got on together the best. Maybe it's because we were that little bit older than the rest and could look upon it all with slightly cynical and jaundiced eyes. The rest of the team were all in their late teens and early twenties and in general seemed like nice kid, but a bit full-on. There was a lot of "we're all having a lot of fun together and we're all best mates forever", but that's a bit harsh I suppose; that's the way kids are at that age and I was probably that way myself twenty or thirty years ago. It was quite funny though to hear them bitching about each other all the time and Steve, Lynn and I wondered what it would be like whenever one of them tripped themselves up.

In general however, it was a bit monotonous. It was a touch of "calm before the storm" because you didn't have to be a genius to work out that Friday and Saturday night may be a bit busier than a Thursday afternoon. It wasn't as if was dead by any means, but we weren't exactly rushed off our feet. From what I recall there was a steady, constant yet not very hectic stream of people asking for cider. And nothing else. Maybe the fact that the bar only sold cider led to a bit of monotony.

I can't recall what I did on my break either; but I think that unlike the Friday and Saturday when I did make a break from the bar for half an hour (or tried to; more of that in a short while), all I did was make myself a cup of tea and sit at the back of the bar with a ciggie, counting the minutes tick by and engaging in inconsequential chatter.

The boredom was broken towards the end of the shift when one of the bar managers from another bar dropped in with some startling news which caused a bit of a hubbub. (I think that is the correct term). It was that much of a hubbub that Phil told us all to stop serving and gather around).

"Right," he said, "This is the situation. One of the other bars has been checked by Trading Standards and we think they've been serving under-age and not checking properly. So just make sure that you are extra cautious and if you're in any doubt at all you must check. Just be very careful and ask me or any of the managers if you aren't sure. Remember that this could cause you to get thrown out so it's in your own interests to be careful." With this admonition ringing in our ears, we got back to the job in hand; i.e. serving over-priced cider to all and sundry (if they looked over 21).

I did actually check a few i/d's and my judgement must have been lacking because everyone was well over the benchmark. Maybe it was my age, but in that weird sort of "don't even policemen look young" way, I had real trouble distinguishing between those who were just over 18 and those who were touching 30. Kids eh? The only way I checked was keeping in my head what the date of birth had to be and cross-checking that against their passport or driving licence. A few of them got a bit uppity when I asked for i/d, but I wasn't really that bothered; if they didn't have any I'd then they didn't get served by me. No doubt they'd chance their arm again with someone else or in another bar, but that wouldn't be my problem. (This next bit may lose me a few readers or at least cause a rating on Amazon to go through the floor, but I do want to give an honest account of what happened so here goes). At one point a scruffy, badly shaven, lanky haired youth approached the bar, swaying gently in the non-existent wind, pupils dilated for England and swearing like a fine one. That didn't cause me any concern; it wasn't as if he particularly stood out from the crowd and I myself was fairly tatty and badly shaven. If I had any hair it would have no doubt been fairly lanky, but at least I wasn't out of my head. I did want to exercise the option of knocking him back however, due to two factors that didn't work in his favour. Firstly, his opening request to me was, "Give me a fucking pint mate". The juxtaposition between the word "fucking" and "mate" was interesting; and I was sorely tempted to respond with "And what's the magic word? Is a "please" too much to ask for?" but I didn't. No, what did it for me was that this fine specimen of humanity staggered up to the bar wearing an Everton FC shirt. Although I'm a lifelong Liverpool fan, I don't have any special animosity towards

Evertonians (more pity than anything else), and I do have some friends that are on the dark side. In some ways I was prepared to forgive this more chap his sartorial mistake and at least chat to a fellow Scouser, but when he repeated his request for a "fucking pint", I was pushed that little bit over the edge. After all, it's only Evertonians who would turn up at Glasto wearing their team shirts. (Here's when I lose readers). This was the excuse I needed.

"Have you got i/d?" I asked.

"Why?" he replied, somewhat incredulously.

"Because you look about 15 years old. Mate." I said. (Not a chance-he was at least 25). He did get the better of me however, because without blinking a (dilated) eye, he produced both a driving licence and a passport.

"Which one do you want to check?"

"Oh both, I think. Got to make sure", I said, and took my time glancing at them. He was well over 18 and I had no choice therefore but to serve him. Didn't get a tip though. Maybe it was because it was just a tad boring; I probably wouldn't have bothered trying to score stupid points if either it was much busier or if there was some variety to the work, but it was just pint after pint of the same stuff. I think that it was at about this point that it dawned on me that even though I hadn't finished my first shift, it was simply a case getting through it, second by second, minute by minute and hour by hour. There was nothing overly difficult about it and on the upside, at least I was at Glastonbury. In fact, there weren't many downsides at all; at least it gave me the chance to see things from another perspective.

While this was all going on, I could see that that ground outside of the bar was getting increasingly muddy, and although it wasn't raining, the combination of footsteps of thousands of people upon already soft ground had obliterated every blade of grass. There didn't seem much prospect of a repeat of the hot weather of the previous year when wearing my Converse instead of a pair of battered sandals seemed somewhat over the top and only really necessary of a night when it got a bit nippy. Wellies seemed to be the order of the day. Even then I didn't realise how muddy that it was getting on the rest of the site, or indeed how much worse it was to become.

Just before the shift finished, Phil called us altogether again. "I've just had a call from Shirley. In fact all the bar managers have had a call. One of the other bars has been caught serving under- age by Trading Standards and it's been shut down. For the rest of the festival. People have been kicked off site and Avalon are going to lose a lot of money. It's not good. Trading Standards are using kids undercover to try to buy alcohol so you must be very careful. From now on, every time you check i/d you must complete this form," he said waving an A4 sheet of paper in front of us. "I'll get some copies and tape it to the bar. You have to write on the sheets what i/d you checked, write and sign your name and tick whether you served them or not. I know it's a pain in the arse, but it has to be done. And it goes without saying because you sign your name, then it's down to you personally."

To me, this half-smacked of Avalon protecting their back at the expense of the staff, but didn't say anything and no-one else seemed to twig. (I thought that some of the crew may have cottoned onto this later, but they all seemed to accept this as the way it had to be. Given my background as a manager in the Civil Service if I'd tried to something like this then there would have been an almighty kick-off, yet these kids seemed blissfully ignorant of any implications for them. Possibly this only crossed my mind as I was that little bit older and a little bit more cynical, but I wasn't going to set any hares running with planting unsubstantiated conspiracy theories. Although looking at it from Avalon's side, then it appeared to be a fairly sensible way to proceed and if I was in their shoes then that's exactly what I would have done.

After this second flurry of excitement, it was nearly all over. The clock ticked closer to 7 o'clock and the other crew started to arrive. My first shift had ended without major incident and I was one third the way through it all. It was time to head back to my temporary home.

Phil offered everyone a free drink at the end of the shift, which most of the young kids took advantage of, but in the best traditions of Sunday tabloids, I made my excuses and left. I was knackered, even though it hadn't been all that busy. I put it down to simply doing something a bit different and the release of all that "will I cope" tension. What I did know, even at this relatively early stage was that I didn't want to see another cider for a long time.

I did feel the need for a coffee however, not having had one since the shift had started. I thought I'd just pop to the nearest coffee stand and grab one for on the way back to the site, but I hadn't reckoned on the sheer difficulty of walking in the mud. Popping anywhere was a bit of a misnomer. It hadn't reached that stage of being the sort of mud that sucked the wellies off your feet without warning or provocation, like some alien life-force; it was more like that sticky winter field-like mud that just slowed you down and made it difficult to move with any sort of speed. Anyway, I did get hold of a coffee and instead of a gentle stroll back to the tent, coffee cup in hand, I sat down for 10 minutes, had a smoke and surveyed the scene. I was too tired really to take it all in. It all seemed a bit of a blur and I realised that I was a bit peckish, not having really eaten much all day. I was starving hungry to be honest and it was that, more than anything that made my mind up. I was going to get back to the site as quickly as I could and get some tea. Although it's easy to get distracted at Glastonbury as there is always so much going on and so much to see-even on a Thursday at just after 7.00 pm when it's not really kicked off-nothing was going to distract me. I was a man on a mission and that mission involved getting something hearty inside me as soon as possible.

Half an hour of plodding later I was back at the site. I made a very quick call home to let everyone know I'd survived, had a quick wash and headed into the mess tent. I would have eaten most things by then, but the best option seemed to be a large plate of pasta with a side order of chips, followed by apple crumble and a few cups of coffee. I got chatting to a few people and before I knew it, time had dragged on. It was dark outside and I glanced at my watch. It was nearly 11.30. I had planned after getting something to eat, to get back down to the festival site and to have a wander around, but I couldn't be bothered with the mud again. I had a late shift the next day and I did really want to see some acts the next day before that. My legs were aching like crazy; probably due to a combination of a) standing up more seven hours straight b) walking to and from the campsite in the mud and c) being generally unfit. (I think that this last element was the most significant factor). Nothing seemed more inviting than crawling into bed and falling fast asleep. As I didn't have a bed per se then a sleeping bag was the next best thing. I got back to the tent, yanked the wellies off, zipped myself up in the sleeping bag and looked at my watch again. It was one minute past midnight and I was going to sleep. Rock and roll.

Chapter 8

Friday is the first day

However much you may read about Tuesday being the new Wednesday or whatever such nonsense about Glastonbury, and irrespective of the fact that I'd been there since Tuesday and spent seven hours working, I still felt somehow that it wouldn't really start properly until the Friday. I still feel that way and I'm not sure why. It may be because not all the stages kick off until the Friday or that it's only broadcast on the BBC from the Friday-or just because it's the weekend. It's totally irrational because most of the people are there from at least the Thursday and just because a few bands jump up on a stage and start thrashing some instruments shouldn't mean it's the signal that it's all started. But that's how it feels to me, in some sort of gut-feeling way.

So, as I slowly woke up on the Friday morning, I was excited in that Christmas-Day-is-finally -here sort of way. This was going to be the day when it all kicked in. I was looking forward to a repeat of the previous years' Friday; blue skies, hot weather, brilliant music, magical times. Granted, Amy wasn't with me and somewhere within the next 24 hours I had to slot in an eight hour shift, but nevertheless, good times were on the way.

I stretched an arm out of the sleeping bag and gently felt the side of the tent with my palm. It was wet, but I expected that; It was just the condensation. It was light outside; I looked at my watch. Twenty past six. The light outside would be the sun just starting to peek through the early summer mist. In that half-asleep/half-awake state I heard a faint patter of condensation running off the outside of the tent. I would have to find where exactly in my rucksack I had put my battered sandals. The wellies would be useless today; but on the other hand if I was going to be on my feet for a significant part of the day, then maybe I should break out the old Converse.

As I came round, it slowly dawned on me (quite a relevant metaphor) that the sound I was hearing wasn't the condensation seeping away from the sides of the tent but something else altogether. Rain. As my head cleared and I became more awake than asleep, I didn't immediately leap into action. I must have laid still in my sleeping bag, listening to this gentle patter for at least ten minutes or so. In a strange way it was quite soothing and a bit like the most ambient music you could imagine. Maybe it wasn't raining at all but instead Eno and Boards of Canada were doing some sort of unannounced secret gig right outside my tent. Or maybe not. Maybe it was just rain and I had to face up to reality. It was good to daydream for a bit, but however much I wished it all away, I knew I had to stick my nose out of the tent and see what exactly was going on. I wriggled myself around and edged towards the front of the tent and, with a certain amount of trepidation, moved the zip down a couple of inches to scan the sky. It was uniformly grey as far as I could see. I pulled the zip down a few more inches, hoping for a break in the clouds somewhat, but there was nothing. It was if a big grey sheet had been thrown over the whole site. In fact there were no clouds at all; it wasn't that threatening, heavy, scudding black clouds sort of view; just a grey sky. The closest way to describe it is as if you went to bed with a colour tv in your front room and in the night it had been mysteriously replaced with a black and white one. This in itself wasn't a bad thing; I'd have liked a touch of blue sky to wake up to, although it wasn't essential. What was certainly not a good thing was the rain, A constant light drizzle. It didn't seem to be a downpour, it wasn't windy, simply steady and continuous. Normally I don't suppose that this would cause much of a problem; if there was such a little shower at home then I think we're all quite used to it and just get on with things. (After all, I'm from the North of England and we have enough practice with rain. It's our default position. Rain). However, 15 minutes of drizzle at Glastonbury is a different proposition altogether. Same cause-but with a very different effect.

It was no good. I had to get out of the tent; at least to nip to the toilet and then on in to get a coffee. At least with an emptier bladder, coffee and nicotine, I'd be able to work out what to do. First off was the wrestle with the wellies; never a particularly easy task, especially when you're in a restricted space and bursting for a piss at the same time. The latter probably assists however, at least in getting them on a bit quicker. I grabbed my ciggies and lighter and exited from the tent, somewhat gracelessly as ever, like a cork from a bottle. Good job that there wasn't any one around to see it. I truly think that it is impossible to look good when getting out of tent.

I slowly stood up and stretched my stiff back. What I saw in front of me was not a pretty sight. Where there had been vestiges of grass all around the tent the previous day; the odd clump of green giving the impression of a field, it had all gone to be replaced by mud. There was the faintest bit of green all around my tent, but even that was only an inch or so. This was due largely because the tent was right at the entrance to the campsite. For everyone and anyone to get to their tents, then they had to pass mine; either to the left or to the right of it. My tent was like a little traffic island at the start of the field. And because everyone had to get past my tent, then the mud all around it was the gloopiest, stickiest and heaviest mud on the whole field. The poor tent looked as if it had been dropped directly into the mud from a great height. It was possibly one of the saddest things I'd ever seen.

It wasn't as if I could do a little hop or skip onto a patch of ground that wasn't muddy, every step of the way from my tent to both the toilets and the mess tent would be a challenge. If I managed to traverse that journey without either losing a welly to the mud and/or falling over sometime in the next few days, then it would be a miracle. With that thought in mind, I gingerly (and successfully), squelched my way first to the toilets and then on to the mess tent where I managed to get a cup of hot coffee. I looked at my watch. It was still only ten to seven. It was so early that the kitchen crew hadn't arrived as yet and there was no clattering of pots and pans in the background and no heady smell of sizzling bacon. There were only a half a dozen hardy souls around and they all looked as if they had either had a very bad night's sleep or hadn't been to bed yet. Whichever way it was, no one seemed to talking, just odd nods and muddy shuffling. This was understandable; I didn't feel like talking either. Instead I grabbed a chair and set it under the awning at the edge of the tent. I watched the raindrops fall from the canvas, put the hood of my hoodie over my head, had a smoke and sipped my coffee.

It was all a bit dispiriting. On the other hand, it wasn't as dispiriting as not being at Glastonbury on a Friday morning in the rain, but being in (normal) work on a Friday morning (in the rain) and knowing that the nearest that I would get to Glastonbury would be switching on the TV after a full days' work and seeing what highlights the BBC had selected. That would have really have put the mockers on things. It was with that little ray of sunshine echoing in my head that prompted me to have a small ironic grin inside and to refresh my coffee. Things are always cheerier with a coffee.

As I rummaged around in my pocket for my lighter, there was my mobile. No need to try to get back to the tent to find it. Time to make a brief call home and find out what things were happening. Although it was only just after 7.00 a.m. everyone would be up. Hopefully. I didn't want to be the early morning alarm call.

Luckily everyone was up and about when I got through and in fact Jackie was able to give me the latest update re the weather from the BBC.

""There will be light rain showers for most of the day and overnight although it should clear by Saturday" ", she quoted, quite breezily. "That sounds ok, doesn't it?"

I wanted to say that it didn't sound ok at all and that the phrase "should clear by Saturday" was a bit sketchy and optimistic to say the least. However, I didn't want it to come out as if I was having a miserable time

(I wasn't) or that I wasn't grateful for her having got up early enough to find out the latest weather forecast. I also didn't want anyone worrying about how the ramshackle tent was holding up or that it seemed that it was possible that it could get completely engulfed in mud within the next 24 hours. So, although I didn't lie as such, I did put a positive spin on things. The tent was fine, there was a bit of mud but not too much, the rain was just going on and off and actually it was that fine and light that I could hardly notice it. I looked up at the grey sky, saw the rain pouring off the canvas as if Michael Eavis himself was standing on the top of the tent throwing buckets of water around, wriggled my wellies around in the couple of inches of mud and wondered if my voice would give it away. I quickly changed the subject by asking how everyone was back home. Thomas was getting ready for work and Amy was fast asleep, so everything was quite normal really. Jackie told me to save the battery on the phone and to ring her later when I knew what I was going to do for the rest of the day. She'd keep me updated with weather forecasts as the day developed.

It would be too early really for breakfast and whilst it was relatively quiet around the campsite, I whittled away half an hour or so by getting to the showers. Just so you don't get the wrong idea I didn't take half an hour in the shower, selfishly using up all the hot water; it was more that it took most of that half hour to get back to the tent and then to the shower and back again to the tent through the mud without any major incident. The ground was getting so difficult to navigate that it did make me think that I should revise my travel time to and from the bar. It was certainly going to be a bit of a slog and longer than the 30 minutes or so I'd reckoned on before.

By the time I'd done all this I was a bit peckish to say the least and the allure of the mess tent was as the top of my mind. When I glooped my way there it was heaving and breakfast servings were in full flow. For once I swerved a coffee and opted for a brew. (It's funny that I refer to a cup of tea as a brew but never a coffee. A coffee is just a coffee). Anyway, this cup of tea was just the thing to accompany a full English, complete with fried bread and the full works. This was better than trying to cook something in the rain and (almost) convinced me of the advantages of working my ticket compared to being a mere punter. My views on this would probably change I thought by the time 7.00 p.m. came around, but at that moment all was good with the world. It was time for a post-breakfast smoke so I grabbed a chair and sat outside the tent once again; it was still raining but just that warm drizzle. Still, that's all that was needed to turn the mud into well, more mud. I got chatting to a couple of fellow social outcasts and as we talked about working, the weather, where we were from and what we planned to do for the rest of the day, the time ticked away. It kind of developed into a sort of coffee relay where we took it turns to replenish each others' drinks. Before I knew it, the time had ticked on past 11.30 a.m. and the first bands were playing on the first day. It had actually kicked off!

But it was raining and it was muddy. The question going around my head was whether I would make the effort to get through the mud and see what was going on or stay nice and dry and warm(ish) by the tent. After mulling this over for a few minutes, there was really no other way to go. So what if I got a tad wet and muddy? I was only there this once and I could always get dry later. My coffee compatriots were all of a mind to hang around the campsite until the rain died off a bit, but being a Northern lad and clearly made of sterner stuff, I zipped up my coat, checked the wellies and said my goodbyes. I felt a bit like Captain Oates heading off into what was an almost certain demise.

I'm sure that it wouldn't have been that much more difficult heading off into a wild, dark Antarctic night than simply trying to get the few hundred yards to the entrance gate. Probably not as deadly, yet difficult nevertheless. Just to get to the gate involved a walk up a steepish path bounded on one side by the big Glasto fence and the other side by chain link fencing at the side of the campsite. Ordinarily, this would have been a grassy path; four days in it was looking like the Cresta Run but comprised of mud rather than ice. There seemed to be two different methods just to get up this path. Some people were trying to walk on the bits of grass that were left right against the fence. The problems with this were that a) these bits of grass were as slippery as fuck because of all the rain and b) it was a thin strip of only about six inches wide so that if you had big feet it was impossible. The other way was just to give it some welly (literally) and try to stomp through the mud as quickly as possible. The problems with this strategy were a) there was a high probability that you'd either fall over and/or lose a welly and b) be so knackered by the time you got to the entrance of the site itself you'd require medical intervention. I tried both methods and they were equally as crap as each other. It took me about 15 minutes to get the couple of hundred yards to the top of the path. I still had to get to the festival entrance itself. What cheered me up just a little bit (but kind of racked with a touch of guilt), was that the path joined up with the main entrance path for ordinary paying punters, all of whom seemed to be covered in mud and so grim-faced that they looked like extras from The Walking Dead. At least I could I have a shower if I wished. These poor souls were trapped in a mud fest for days. (I did feel bad about even thinking this. It was quite ironic in a sort of "be careful what you wish for" way. After all, nine months ago I had been cursing my luck about not getting hold of a ticket and here I was counting my blessings. If I had actually got a ticket, then I would have been just another of the doomed and damned, shuffling my miserable way to the gates).

And they did, by and large, all look generally miserable. Most of them were lugging rucksacks and all their camping gear and I figured that these were people who either by accident or design, could only have got to Glasto on the Friday. Goodness knows where they were going to put their tents up as the whole site had seemed fairly full the day before. The thought of this, combined with the constant summer rain and foul mud, was probably going through their minds as well and causing the big sad faces. I noticed one couple gamely trying to push a stroller pram, complete with a crying toddler in it. The wheels were totally jammed with mud and not moving at all. I couldn't think of anything more futile. One bloke had a wheelbarrow stacked with cases of cider, which, as I looked on, decided to shed its wheel and collapse in a heap. The whole thing resembled what I imagined Napoleon's retreat from Moscow must have been like, except that it was a little bit warmer.

By the time I got to the gate I did find myself wondering if it had been all worth it. Maybe I'd have been better off just staying in the mess tent and drinking coffee all day. However, I'd made it this far and it seemed a bit daft just to turn on my (muddy) heels and head on back. Furthermore, one of the advantages of being "crew" was that I could jump the queue and head straight through the gates.

Wristbands duly tugged and checked, I skipped through the turnstiles; metaphorically of course-it was too muddy to skip anywhere and even if it wasn't, my days of skipping anywhere were long behind me and I would have looked ridiculous. As it happened, I suppose that I didn't appear as the epitome of cool anyway. At this stage, as ever, comfort and warmth won the day over style.

Once through the gates there was an extremely lethal and odd puddle to traverse before heading towards the rest of the festival site. It was more like a small pond rather than a puddle and there was literally no way around it as it stretched the full width of the field as you got through the gates. It was the colour and consistency of hot chocolate, but was a bit colder. It was hard to judge how deep it was and it was only by gauging how far it went up people's wellies as they struggled through it that I could tell. It was the oddest thing though, not exactly muddy and just like a pond. Although I saw many varieties of mud at Glastonbury that year, I never came across anything like this anywhere else. Plenty of sticky mud, gloopy mud, slimy mud, muddy mud yet nothing like this Ovaltinely horror . (Oh, how quickly I became an expert on such matters. That's what Glasto is all about-forget all the music, good times, reckless hedonism and the like; mud-spotting is the way to go kids).

I watched people carrying their rucksacks, cases of cider, tents, prams and children over their heads as they gingerly walked through the pond. It was like some surreal outtake from a Vietnam movie and instead of soldiers wading through the minor tributaries of the Mekong Delta with their rifles over their heads, here I was observing Glastonbury grunts doing something very similar. Maybe Oliver Stone could do a Glastonbury film. Or Coppola-"the horror, the horror" etc. I took the puddle/pond with care, exchanging rueful glances with others, just in case anyone fell over, but luckily no-one slipped or splashed and it was some relief that I got through to a bit of drier ground. If I had been a normal Glasto-goer then I would have had to get to the Pyramid by walking down a long muddy path, but being a worker, I was directed through a gate that led to a flat, straight, gravelled service road which took me to the top of the hill by the Pyramid.

Strolling along that road in relative isolation, without any mud underfoot and just the gentle patter of rain on the trees above, convinced me that I'd done the best thing. I had the best intentions of at least seeing the opening act on the Pyramid, but time hadn't worked in my favour and in any event, it all felt a bit too soggy and somewhat inappropriate for the Master Musicians of Joujouka. Desert music did not seem to be the order of the day. Although I could see a certain irony in standing in a muddy field in Somerset alongside a few hundred others wearing rain ponchos listening to a bunch of chaps pluck various obscure and arcane stringed instruments and singing in a language that

I'm sure no-one understood about the beauty and glory of the rolling dunes of the Sahara (at least I think that was what they would have been on about), I had spent too long gabbing back at the mess tent and by the time I'd got anywhere near the front of the Pyramid, the said Master Musicians had long gone. I'd wager they were backstage, having changed out of their flowing desert clothes and were lolling around in wellies and Barbours, glugging their way through an extensive rider and chuckling to each other at the silly English people getting wet and cold. So I missed out on them, but did manage to catch the last couple of songs by Metronomy. Catch in the sense of catching a dose of the flu. Possibly I wasn't as much at the cutting edge as I had imagined but there seemed nothing vaguely attractive, interesting or challenging about Metronomy. From a distance in the rain, they appeared to be some sort of sub- XX outfit, but leaping and running around the stage with a certain amount of angst. Something had upset them because a lot of grimacing was going on. They did seem to be going down rather well with the audience but, despite that, it all kind of left me cold. What kind of put the tin hat on it for me was an underlying hint of Muse. I am sure that I was giving them a bit of a disservice and that they weren't really that bad. After all, I hadn't ever heard them before and just a couple of songs in the rain early on a Friday afternoon at Glastonbury maybe wasn't the best introduction. They did come across as a bit intense, but in that sort of studied intensity where accusations of insincerity can be bandied around quite easily.(Like now). However, it had been at least 45 minutes since I had last had any caffeine so I was well due a coffee and a sit down out of the rain; which had carried on relentlessly since I'd got up at 6.30 in the morning.

There were plenty of stalls selling coffee within spitting distance of where I was, but I really needed to find somewhere where I could sit down and get undercover as opposed to standing in the rain and watching my coffee get gradually diluted with rainwater. Irrespective of the coffee (never an easy thing for me to consider), I just felt as if I needed to get out of the rain. It was reaching that point when I could feel that it was starting to seep through all the tiny gaps in my coat. There's shower proof, rainproof and waterproof; and although there was no label in the jacket to confirm which one of these three categories it fell into, I had the distinct impression that it was the former rather than the latter. There were damp patches starting to form in places that they shouldn't. Although that was something that I realise would happen to me sooner, rather than later, considering that I was on the wrong side of 50, I did know that it was simply something to do with the incessant rain as opposed to an underlying medical condition. Or so I hoped. Anyway, a coffee and shelter was what I really needed. The time warped warblings of the Wu Tang Clan on the Pyramid was something that I could do without.

It wasn't easy finding somewhere that both served coffee and had somewhere to shelter as well as being able to sit down. There were plenty of stalls selling coffee and a few of them did have little awning things. However, all of those with awnings were crammed with huddled masses, sheltering from the rain. Everyone looked liked damp sparrows roosting in trees. I think that it was possibly due to the fact that I hadn't had any caffeine for a good while, but it seemed to me that there was a close resemblance between the soggy punters and the birds in the old

Roobarb cartoon. (This may be a 1970's reference too far, but if you look it up on the net then you'll see what I'm driving at). I stomped through the mud like a lizard with a grudge trying to find somewhere that had all the three things that I was looking for; coffee, cover and somewhere to rest my wearying bones. It was as if I was wandering through a desert, completely lost and hoping to find the oasis just over the brow of the next sand dune but to no avail. I was just about to give it up, because I knew that the further I struggled through the mud, then the further I was getting away from the campsite and therefore the further I would have to go to get back, potentially coffee-less, and the whole thing would have been a waste of time. But like waiting for a bus that never arrives, I knew that if I gave up the hunt and turned on my (muddy) heels, then surely there would have been just what I'd been looking for a few yards away, just around the corner.

So I stuck with it and, looking at my watch, I thought I'd give it just another 5 minutes. I'd go as far as the John Peel Stage and if I hadn't found anything by then, I'd give it up as a bad job and head on back. As I got closer this self-imposed limit of my epic trek, I saw what I thought must have surely been a mirage. If it hadn't been raining that hard. I stopped and rubbed my eyes in disbelief. There, close to the tent, was what appeared to be bit of a place serving food and drinks, complete with benches and tables covered from the elements by a canvas roof. It was up a bit of a slope, which, in the best of times, would have been a touch of a climb, even for someone in fine physical shape..

Now the slope was the equivalent of a particularly dangerous ride at a theme park. Abandoned wellies littered the sides and as I watched, at least three people slipped at the top and tumbled on their arses, all the way to the bottom. It all seemed like great fun to them, but I was fully intending to keep hold of my wellies and what little dignity that I had left and get to the coffee without falling over. I gingerly headed up the slope, carefully planting my feet in what looked like previous footprints. (Lest I make this sound over dramatic, it wasn't exactly as if I was scaling the North Face of the Eiger. The total length of the slope must have only been twenty yards or so yards and although it was steep-ish, that's all it was, steep-ish). It still took me a good few minutes to get to the top and into the café. I shook the rain from my jacket and slumped against the counter. I ordered a cappuccino and as I took the first sip, I must have looked like John Mills in "Ice Cold in Alex". Except that I wasn't in the desert and I didn't look as cool. Still, it was good as a cold lager, if not better. I wandered over to a table and finally managed to sit down. This was the life.

This was the life, even as I sat huddled away from the rain and nursing a coffee. I looked at my watch again and thought even with all this rain and mud, that it was infinitely better being at Glastonbury than it would be being back in work on a Friday afternoon. Glastonbury gives me that "away from it all feeling" that you get on holiday, that "it's all another world away and whatever is happening back there doesn't really matter", but to a much greater degree. Now this isn't a result of me being off my head at Glastonbury in any way, shape or form. I know that there are countless number of people who go to Glastonbury and have either the "what happens at Glasto stays at Glasto" or the whole "I totally re-evaluated my life" experience. I am sure that for some people it is a life-changing experience and that they head off to do something wholly unexpected- and that for some others a weekend of drink, drugs and debauchery stays 100% behind the fence in Somerset.

On the other hand, and being somewhat cynical, I am sure that the vast majority who go through this at Glastonbury head on back on the Monday morning to their usual lives and forget that over consumption of mind-altering substances (either legal or not) caused immense amounts of bullshit to be spilled during the preceding few days. I do recognise that this lends a slight air of puritanism to my stance on this point at the very least. This is particularly pointed as the strongest thing that passes my lips at Glastonbury is black coffee and too many cigarettes. There have been many times in the past that I've spouted complete nonsense due to one too many pints of Guinness and the fact that I don't really drink that much now hasn't stopped the flow of bollocks that I can come out with at times. I can readily talk shite when stone-cold sober. I'm not really bothered when people swear blind that they are totally going to do something different with their lives after being at Glastonbury (usually I hear this when they are swaying in the breeze and staring intently at me), and if anything, I find it quite funny. The whole point of this is that in some ironic way going to Glastonbury myself over the past four years has changed me in some way, but I'm not exactly sure how and to what extent. I'm not getting all mystical here at all and I don't think it's got anything at all to do with mysterious forces, ley-lines or crystals; all I can put it down to is simply that I'm somewhere completely different to my usual life back home and mixing with and talking with people who I wouldn't normally be with.

Whichever way it is, it does cause me every time I'm there to slightly re-evaluate things but not in any deep sort of way, just kind of sub-consciously at the back of my mind. I do know that if I hadn't ever gone to Glastonbury then I wouldn't have started writing with any sort of intent. (At this point many people will be wishing that I'd never managed to get that ticket). All these sort of thoughts were playing in my head as I finished my coffee and looked out of the café at the rain still falling.

It was time to head on back. Or maybe not. Maybe time for another coffee; I was sure I could squeeze another one in. After all, it seemed a bit of shame to get all that way and only have one drink. I was tad peckish as well and the big slices of cake looked fairly tempting. I didn't have to think too long about it and a few minutes later I was merrily finishing off a slab of carrot cake with a large cappuccino to hand. It was still raining, but in my heart the sun was shining. That's all it takes really, a piece of cake and a coffee. And a ciggie. I rummaged in my pocket for my lighter and lit up. Well, I tried to but all that happened was a damp click. I knew that buying a packet of five lighters form Poundstretchers wasn't really the best investment; pay peanuts, get monkeys etc. This was the second lighter that had given up the ghost at an early stage and a third had a flame so evil that it nearly had taken my eyebrows off. A 60% failure rate isn't too good. Possibly some higher power was telling me that I should give up smoking. However, that higher power intervened in another way as the bloke sitting next to me kindly offered me a light. (That's the problem with believing in higher powers; you never know quite where you are with them. One minute they are giving you a sign that you should go in one direction, and the next it's something wholly contradictory). Sitting in the rain and sharing a light with someone generally seems to lead to a conversation, especially at Glastonbury and in this instance, it was no exception. So smoking is not a wholly bad thing then, I suppose?

As British people tend to do, we started chatting about the weather and the general conditions on site. This was his first time at Glastonbury and he'd come down from somewhere in the North East with his partner who was slipping and sliding her way over to the table with a couple of hot drinks in her hands. I really should have had my notebook with me, but I can't recall their names, even though we introduced ourselves and shook hands. A very British thing to do as well, but maybe something that you don't do every day with complete strangers, unless you're at Glasto.

Anyway, I'd guess that they were in their late thirties and over the next half hour or so the conversation ranged from what bands and artists we all wanted to see, where they were camped, how long it had taken them to get there, what we all did for a living and of course, the rain. Which was still falling steadily, but it was nothing more than a drizzle.

"So, how are you coping with all this?" I asked, waving my hand towards the sky.

"Well, it's just a bit of rain," he laughed, "We can handle this, we're Northerners!"

His partner grimaced a touch at this point.

"Oh the rain's ok, I suppose," she said, "But the mud. And the toilets! There are some right dirty bastards around aren't there?"

I had to agree with them and told them of my tales of Amy's numerous and close encounters with the Glasto toilets the previous year.

"I don't know what's worse-when it's hot or when it's muddy", I said.

"Whatever the weather's like, I bet they're always bad," she said.

"What's it like round your tent?" I asked, changing the subject. (After all, there's only so much you can say about the toilets at Glasto).

"Oh, it's alright" he said, "We got here on Wednesday morning and we found somewhere fairly quiet over there." He pointed somewhere up the hill, behind the café. I guessed that it was pretty close to the family field where we'd camped in 2010. "It's pretty muddy but the tent's holding up well." They both looked like the sort of people who would be handy with putting a tent up, unlike myself. I wondered if my Asda contraption would have popped down of its own accord during the past couple of hours.

"So where have you camped?" she asked.

I told them all about not being able to get tickets and therefore ending up working (not good) and my camping site, complete with clean-ish toilets, hot showers and hot food (pretty good).

"I suppose the main thing is though," I asked, "Are you enjoying it? Was it worth it all?"

"Oh yes," he said, "It's been brilliant so far and it's not really started yet. Most people seem so friendly, it's a great atmosphere. Wish we done this earlier."

"We always meant to," she explained, "But we never got around to doing it and other things just got in the way, you know, work and stuff. This year, though we decided we had to stop talking about it and give it a try."

"You'd do it again then?" I said.

"Well, even with all this shitty weather, it's been good and it can't be like this every year, so I think we really will."

I'd finished my coffee a while ago and knew that time was moving on and therefore I had to as well. Work called etc. They were such a friendly couple and it was so good to chat with some fellow Northerners, even though they were from the other side of the Pennines. (We never even talked about football either; I'm sure if we had I'd have spent another hour or so with them). I said my goodbye and wished them all the best for the rest of the weekend. I hope they had a good time. I'm sure they did; they seemed such hardy folk that a touch of mud wouldn't have phased them that much.

I wandered out into the drizzle and zipped my jacket up to my neck. I wasn't going to mess around at this point. The plan was to get straight back to the tent, make sure that it hadn't degenerated into a sodden lump of nylon, have something to eat and get ready for my 7 p.m. shift. I wasn't going to stop for anything and get distracted. Simply get back to the campsite as quickly as possible; no hesitation, no quick coffees or even bottles of water. I did however, buy a lighter from the first stall that I could; I wasn't going to go without the chance of having a smoke on the way back, and there was always a chance that the two lighters I had left in the tent could have been washed away. Get my priorities right; just be able to have a smoke. It wouldn't have mattered if everything else had been destroyed or if all my spare clothes and sleeping bag were lying in a muddy puddle. At least I'd be able to survey the wreckage with the comfort of nicotine. But apart from that brief pit stop it was full throttle all the way back. I would have jogged back if I was a) anyway fit enough (see smoking and carrot cake reference above by way of explanation) and b) if the ground hadn't turned into something close to sticky Play Dough.

Even during the hour or so I'd spent at the café, the mud had got a lot worse. I suppose it was a due to a combination of so many people moving around and the constant rain, but every step had to be considered carefully. It was knackering. Not just the sheer physical effort of moving through the mud-and that's what it was, moving through it, like wading through treacle-but the stressful concentration of making sure that each step you took didn't end up in the loss of a welly or falling over in some sort of You've Been Framed out take. I was determined to get back without that happening but each step was like undertaking an mini Heath and Safety risk assessment in my head.

I bypassed the Pyramid with nary a glance at BB King's show bizzy Vegas-style blues, not breaking a stride. It was quite ironic I guess, I'm sure that I heard the phrase "blues falling down like rain" drifting through the air. I stopped to catch my breath by the time I got to the top of the field and looked down towards the Pyramid Stage. Because it was fairly high up, the rain gave the appearance more of a misty morning than a drizzly Friday afternoon. It was quite pretty and almost moved me to poetry. Almost, until I glanced at the ground. "Sod poetry", I thought to myself. "Just got to get back to the site."

It should have taken about 10 minutes in normal conditions, but half an hour later I slipped and slided my way without disaster through the exit gate and back into the site. The first thing I looked for was a mass of tangled grey nylon lying on the ground just beyond the mess tent. That what would have remained of my tent. But to my utter surprise, I could see that it was still intact and hadn't collapsed. It looked pretty much as it had when I left earlier. On opening it, I did expect that it would have sprung at least one leak, but it was as dry as a bone inside. Maybe my camping skills were not as bad or as inept as I had thought. More by accident than by design though. I think that the fact it had neither fallen over nor leaked was simply that Asda make such a good product for less than £50. But that's probably due more to accident than anything else as well and it had only coped with a bit of rain so far. No downpours or driving winds.

With these cheery thoughts in mind, I nipped down to the mess tent for something to eat. But it was a bit early for a meal yet, taking into account that I would be doing an 8 hour shift and that it would be a long time before I got something substantial down me. There was time for a coffee and a quick phone call home however. I looked around the mess tent but there wasn't anyone I recognised in there as I got a brew and in any event the evening food wasn't going to get served for an hour or so. Now I had (another) coffee to hand, I grabbed a chair and sat in now what was my usual spec it's strange how quickly you become institutionalised-and pulled my phone from my jacket. By keeping it switched off it had retained its charge quite well but it was that old that it took a few minutes to fully boot up. So me and my phone had something in common-fairly old, not the latest version and takes a while to fully spark up. A fitting match. While it was creaking into life, I tried to get the mud off my wellies. No wonder I was so knackered; there was so much sticking to them that it had been as if I'd been walking around with a small child strapped to my legs.

"Hello! How's it going?" It was great to hear Jackie's voice on the phone, clear as a bell. Although I'm not a major aficionado of mobile phones, at times like that, it does make me understand how useful they are. It did make me wonder how on earth things got sorted at Glastonbury before there were mobiles. Not just for anyone attending the festival as punters and trying to get in touch with each other or just phoning home, but all the organising beforehand, setting up and the like. Of all the changes that's happened around the festival in the past 20 years or so, I'd wager that this has been the one that has made the most difference; and the single thing that has made it the fairly well-oiled event it is now. Without mobiles I guess there'd still be long queues of people waiting to use pay phones (what are "payphones" Dad?) and Annie Lennox and Paul Young would be headlining the Pyramid. Isn't technology wonderful? (Most people who don't know me will be wondering why I hadn't taken the simple option of texting home throughout the day to find out how things were. I am possibly the worst person at texting on the world. It would have taken me at least 10 minutes simply to compose any message that made sense and even then I probably would have deleted it by mistake before sending it. I have a real blind spot as far as mobiles are concerned; I'm like a refugee from a TV advert for life assurance i.e. here's a simple phone anyone over the age 80 can use, there's only one button to press, no medical is required and you get a free pen just for applying).

"Well, it's going well, all things considered. How's things back home?"

"Everyone's fine and wondering how you're doing?"

I filled her in with all the exciting details of the day, the mud and the coffee, the carrot cake and the amazing fact that the tent was still up. It was all very rock and roll.

"Anyway," she said, "I won't stay on too long, 'cos you'll want to save your battery. Do you want to know what the forecast is saying now? I've just looked and it says "heavier rain and winds through to Saturday morning then drying up" What's it like now?"

"Oh, it's just that drizzle that's been going on all day and.." As if on cue, the sky suddenly turned darker and the canvas on the mess tent began blowing and flapping noisily behind me. "Oh, bollocks!" Big fat rain drops started pelting everywhere. It was as if some had turned a heavenly tap on. "You're a bloody jinx!" I said, "I'm going to have to get in out of this rain. I'll ring you later before I do my shift. Bye!" And with that I scurried in to the tent, dragging the chair behind me. It was raining that hard now that sheltering at the edge of the tent wasn't going to work. It was coming down like stair rods.

I stood at the door of the mess tent and watched it coming down. It all seemed a bit grim. Jackie had said that the forecast was for this to end by the next morning. Well, for eight of those intervening hours I'd be working and it would be better that if the weather was going to be dreadful sometime during the weekend, then for it to be like that would be best when I was trapped behind the bar. Every cloud had a silver lining, but not those that were scudding across the sky. They were uniformly dark grey, heavy and threatening.

People were running out of the rain and past me into the mess tent. It struck me as quite funny because nearly all of them shook their arms as they got inside and dry. They were like dogs jumping out of a bath.

I was sort of marooned in there while the rain fell, but at least I could see my tent from the doorway and it was holding up well. I didn't exactly know what I would have done if it had blown away or collapsed under the weight of the rain as I had nothing to make any emergency repairs, except for a roll of gaffa tape and I don't know what use that would have been.

Everyone had suddenly seemed to have the one idea - to get out of their tents and into the mess tent. It was getting very full and with that rainy, summery, soggy, warm and sweaty atmosphere, I didn't think that it would end up being the most pleasurable experience in a few hours.

There was already quite a long queue forming for the food, so I thought I'd better not wait too long before I got something to eat, just in case that the only option that would be left would have been something totally vegetarian. I didn't think that I could keep going all the way through an evening shift simply with a plate of lentil casserole or such other pulse and bean type concoction. I picked up a tray and stood dutifully in line. It was a bit like being back at school again.

And it was like being back at school again. I polished off a plate of pasta bolognaise (that wasn't too much like my school-a bit too exotic for late 60's Lancashire school dining) but chips as well (always chips!) and swiftly followed up with a huge slice of jam roly poly and thick custard (how much more school-dinnery can it have got?)

I was in a world of my own as I sat back in the chair, full up with stodgy yet perfect food. It may have been dreadful weather outside but inside (my stomach at least) everything was pure contentment. Just like it is after a full Christmas dinner, I could feel myself nodding off. I could have done with a nap and could have quite easily fallen fast asleep there and then. This was quite astonishing because there were so many people in the tent, with barely a spare seat, and just like a school dinner hall, it was getting louder and louder. It wouldn't have been too unexpected if a head-teacher had jumped up at the front and told us all to be quiet or if a dinnertime bell had gone off and there had been a grumbly shuffle towards the door. I wondered if I could get seconds of the jam roly-poly. These are the sort of stray thoughts that you get in your mind just as you are drifting off to sleep. I would have been in the Land of Nod within seconds, despite all the clatter, if I hadn't felt a tap on my shoulder. I jumped a bit out of my chair to find Steve standing beside me with a tray of food.

"Alright!" he said, "How are you doing?"

"Christ, I'm knackered. Good job you've turned up, I was just dropping off. Here you are, sit down, there's a spare seat over there. " I got up and moved what was one of the only few empty chairs over."Are you ok for a brew?" I asked, "I'm just going to get one."

"Yeah, ok, grab me a coffee then, cheers."

I snaked my way to and from the urns through the assorted soggy throngs and caught up with what Steve had been doing all day. Like myself, he'd wandered around the site and ended up spending most of the afternoon in the acoustic tent, where he'd seen John Otway and Newton Faulkner (not on the stage at the same time. I didn't think so anyway). Newton Faulkner wasn't (and still isn't) my cup of tea at all, but Steve seemed to have enjoyed it. Each to their own, I guessed, although a couple of coffees and a slice of carrot cake would always beat 2011's equivalent of Mick Hucknall to the punch.

But as you do, we chatted more about the weather and the general conditions of the site i.e. the mud, rather than the merits of the flame-haired galoot. We'd just got into whether the weather would have any effect at all on how busy the bar would be during our evening shift when Lynn spotted us both and managed to squeeze into the only spare chair on the table. She plonked her tea tray down.

"Well, what have you two been up to all day?" she asked quite breezily, all things (the mud and the rain) being considered. Steve gave her a potted update about the acoustic tent and I mumbled something vague about stomping through the mud for a coffee and a slice of cake. It didn't sound very rock and roll and wasn't something that I couldn't have done anywhere else. Maybe I should have put a gloss on things and said that I'd spent the afternoon getting wasted drinking cider and smoking weed with a bunch of crusties, but that's not really my style; I'm clearly more of a caffeine and cake sort of chap. "And what did you get up to?" I asked.

"Well," she said, in between eating mouthfuls of chips, "I went up to the Healing Fields and saw what was happening; it was really good, even though it took me ages and ages to get there." Now, I've always wondered myself about the Healing Fields myself and ordinarily (i.e. outside of Glasto) I would have run a mile from what I would dismiss as new age hippy bollocks (here my faux 76/77 punk credentials come to the fore), but I really should give it a look sometime. After all, it might be better than I could possibly imagine.

However much the idea of seeing the Healing Fields was a good one in theory, in practice I didn't go in 2011. Or 2013. And possibly I will never go. When Lynn started telling us all about it, I ended up a bit like Homer Simpson concentrating on something he has no interest in or comprehension of. All I heard was "..crystals...healing...lovely..amazing...relaxing...peaceful....". My mind was in another place altogether. (Maybe I really did need to get to the Healing Fields to sort out my mind-focussing issues out). I think that

Steve was moving in the same direction as I was, although we both nodded along politely, neither of us seemed overly enthusiastic. Yet Lynn appeared to have had a good day herself and I supposed we were both pleased for her. In any event it's always better to work alongside someone who is happy rather than grumpy. We all had eight hours of sheer fun ahead of us, we all needed to be in that happy place.

The conversation moved on to what we all thought it would be like that evening and what we were expecting. The consensus was that if the rain carried on in the same vein as it had done for the past hour or so, then it would all be pretty quiet. I was hoping not; there's nothing much worse than working a bar when it's dead. All you can do is wander around collecting and cleaning glasses to while away the time. Even that option wasn't open; there was no point in washing paper cups.

By the time Lynn had finished her meal and we'd all had another brew it was getting time to move. Well, for me, it was time to move slightly outside, dodging the rain to have a (damp) ciggie. Lynn pottered off back to her tent and Steve headed off for a shower. Well, he queued up in the rain for a shower. It seemed a bit of a pointless exercise to me. It was raining that hard he may as well just stood in the field with a bottle of shampoo and to let Mother Nature take her course. We chatted for a few minutes in the pouring rain.

"This seems like total waste of time!" I said. "Look at it, you are going to get as wet, if not wetter, by standing here instead of getting into the shower."

We watched people getting into the showers, looking wet, muddy and dishevelled and saw them coming out looking wet and dishevelled. The only difference as that there seemed to be slightly less muddy. And in one instance, just as muddy. One chap stepped out of the shower block, took a couple of steps and went completely arse over tit, towel flying in one direction and shower gel, razor and shampoo another. People jumped in to help him out, but in his embarrassment he got up, covered in mud and walked back towards the tents as if he actually intended to do this as soon as he'd had his shower. It was just like when you trip up in the street; you have to pretend that you meant to do it and carry on as normal. I would have done exactly the same.

Steve and I looked at each other. "Not sure if it's worth getting a shower now," he said, "Think I'll give it a miss after seeing him."

"See you back at the bar then?" I said. We headed back to our respective tents through the rain and the wind.

As I unzipped my tent and checked it for leak damage (none so far), it crossed my mind that it seemed a long time ago-much more than a year- that I was sitting outside the tent with Amy and Sacha in the blazing sun and making sure that the tent stayed open as long as possible in order that it didn't turn into some sort of greenhouse. It was one of those little moments that hit hard sometimes and quite out of the blue; I wished that Amy was with me then and that I wasn't on my own. She would have either really hated the rain and the wind and would have moaned constantly or shrugged it off and told me not to be such a wimp. Just the thought of that made me smile to myself. She'd be a right laugh one way or another in this weather. But I had to get sorted and down to the bar before all the large t-shirts went, so musing on hypothetical situations would have to wait. I checked all the seams on the tent and that there was nothing that I really needed close to the edges just in case it did leak while I was working. The words "in case" were a tad optimistic as I fully expected it to be waterlogged by the time I got back. I gave home a quick ring before I headed off into the rain again; Amy was out, but I guessed that wasn't a bad thing-I possibly would have considered about swerving the shift if I'd spoken to her. I had a brief chat with Thomas and sort of skirted around with Jackie about the rain. I promised I'd ring back in the morning, unzipped the tent and headed off to work.

That seemed like an odd concept, going to work at Glastonbury, but that was what it was to me. It was strange that only after doing one shift I was considering it as work and that by the end of the night I would be two thirds the way through my commitment. Maybe that was the only way or the best way to deal with it; just to consider it as work, nothing more and nothing less. I commuted my way to the bar therefore at a great pace, not being distracted by anything on the way, not even the ridiculous posturing of Biffy Clyro on the Pyramid. When I say at a great pace, well, all that is relative. This was at a pace that was governed by how quickly I could get through the crowds and the mud i.e. not very quickly. I was given a bit of impetus however; thanks to Biffy Clyro I sped up somewhat and reached the bar in record time-it only took me half-an-hour or so.

I got there in time to see that the bar was surprisingly busy; which was a good thing. Everyone was busy working behind the bar and I seemed to be the first one of my team to arrive. There was no-one else at the back of the bar except me and the two chaps who ran all the techie stuff for the cider to get through to the bar; gas cylinders, big kegs of cider and numerous pipes and tubes, switches and cabling. It all seemed quite complex to me and a million miles away from the first bar I ever worked in. That had hand pulled pints from wooden barrels and none of this new-fangled computerised thingys. (It was all fields around here etc. Actually it is all fields around Glastonbury as well so I don't really know what the point is). Anyway, the two chaps were busy switching switches and the like and just nodded hello to me as I walked in, then carried on with their techie work.

Because I had arrived relatively early and was in the backstage area by myself, I had time to rummage through the increasingly tatty box of t-shirts and find one that was marked large. Still no xl however. I'd had a false hope that one would show up but all that was there was large and small. Maybe everyone else was a medium. (In a t-shirt rather than psychic way). I held up two large t shirts side by side to see if one was slightly bigger than the other, but in that infuriating way that sometimes the that the little things never work out, they were exactly the same size. I tried stretching one of them before anyone walked in but there didn't seem too much give in it. "Ah! Fuck it!" I muttered, "It'll have to do." I stretched the shirt as much as I possibly could and whipped it on. I saw that it fitted in all the right places i.e. everywhere. There wasn't much room for manoeuvre. Having said that, it wasn't meant to be a fashion item (as if) and at least with it being so snug at least I would stay warm. It did feel even smaller than the one I'd worn the previous day, but I was sure that the carrot cake wasn't that fattening. I'd completed the switch from my own comfy, baggy shirt to the figure-hugging one in near isolation and thus avoided any potential embarrassment. I'd have bet that none of the team, all being generally fit, lithe and skinny as fuck, would have been searching for the biggest t shirt possible before they started their shift. They could have worn the first thing that they pulled out of the box and it would have been ok. For me, the perils of having what may be euphemistically termed as a "stocky frame" should not be underestimated.

Because I'd arrived at the bar in double-quick speed I'd not only had time to carefully hand pick a t shirt, but also to boil a kettle and make a cup of tea. It strikes me as odd in retrospect that amidst all the frenetic activity around Glastonbury, and especially at the back of a busy bar on the Friday night, that I was all by myself, in isolation, quietly squeezing a tea bag and sipping strong tea from a chipped mug, wondering what the next shift would bring. Sometimes it was good to have a cup of tea rather than a coffee. It wasn't exactly quiet as I could hear through the door of the bar that the music was really loud. All this peace didn't last long, as within minutes other members of the team started to arrive in dribs and drabs and as I expected, they all nonchalantly stuck their hands in the box and miraculously picked out exactly the right t shirts for themselves. None of that stretching and pulling for them.

The door of the bar opened and Phil stuck his head around. "Hi!" he shouted above the hubbub, "You all ok? Are you ready in about ten minutes? It's busy in there so get yourselves a cup of tea if before you start. I'll catch up with you all in a minute to let you know what's happening." I glanced through the open door and it was busy. The bar was heaving, about three deep all the way round and the team that were working looked knackered. You could tell it had been busy because they were stepping over sleeves of unused paper cups that had fallen to the floor that clearly nobody had time to pick up. This was all a good thing. I just hoped that it would stay as busy as this for the following eight hours. The shift would be over before I knew it, I'd squeeze in my break and nip to see at least a bit of U2 and if I was knackered, then at least I'd sleep like a log. I could see from the reactions of the rest of the team that they weren't exactly enamoured of the idea of a busy night. I could feel myself turning into a grumpy (or even a grumpier than usual) old man. "These kids don't even know the meaning of hard work" etc. I decided to keep my opinions to myself, discretion being the better part and asked a couple of them what they'd been up to all day. It all seemed to have revolved around getting up late and getting pissed. In the rain. Not my cup of tea but there you go-I nodded indulgently and got back to swilling off my cup of tea. Steve and Lynn had turned up, fresh- faced and ready to go.

"These t-shirts are crap, aren't they?" Steve moaned. He was only a shirt bloke, but what he lacked in height, he made up with in girth. He looked as uncomfortable in his as I felt in mine.

"And I don't know how many people have worn these before us," Lynn sniffed, "This one is a bit wiffy."

"Don't think that it's a priority for them," I replied. "But after a few days everything here gets wiffy."

Our debate regarding the relative merits of the t-shirts was cut short when Phil popped back from the bar.

"Ok, ok everyone, you all ready to go in a minute?" He shouted above the noise and there was a general sound of sushing. "Everyone here? Good. This is what's happening tonight. There's a couple of bands on in a bit and we've got some Mexican wrestling later." He let that one sink in for a second. He had perfect comedic timing as he said it completely deadpan. Mexican wrestling? There was no time for anyone to question this as he carried on. "It's really busy so we'll have two people running the tills and two people pulling the drinks for now. The rest of you can take the orders. OK?"

He looked at me and Steve, "You two alright for the drinks?" We nodded. It was fine with me. He picked two others for the tills. "Let's go" he said, and we walked through to the bar.

Bang! And then it started. No time to settle down into anything. The last team squeezed past us with that "you're fucking welcome to it" sort of look in their eyes, but there wasn't a chance to more than nod hello before it all kicked in. It was heaving. I stood by the machine, pulled the lever, pressed the button for 12 pints at a time, non-stop for an hour and a half. It was relentless. As soon as I had a dozen pints pulled then they were whipped away and I was onto the next 12. It was all very mechanical and I managed to get quite a rhythm going. Cups, lever, button, lever, button, done. Cups, lever, button, lever, button, done.

Cups, lever, button, lever, button, done. I built up quite a rhythm to it all; similar to any sort of repetitive task such as photocopying a stack of papers or painting a fence. (I know; I'm making all this seem very exciting. Go to Glastonbury and it's the equivalent of painting a fence). However, that's the way it was and there wasn't really much time for anything else. I sort of zoned out from it all and only concentrated upon keeping the pints going in a steady stream. I didn't even look around to see how busy it was, even though it must have been by the sheer amount of cider that was flowing. Every so often I glanced up to see Steve doing exactly the same with his machine.The only time I moved was when the supply ran out and I had to shout to the back for the chaps to switch barrels. Actually, I don't think there was anything as quaint as barrels; it was more like tanks, but whichever it was it only took them 30 seconds or so to get the industrial-type liquid flowing again. These brief respites allowed me to grab more sleeves of cups to set up and I was off again. I was that much into the whole process that I didn't notice how noisy (or quiet) it was or the sheer freneticism all around me.

The only thing that stood out was seeing the till-which was right next to the machine- constantly opening and closing and an incessant ring ring ring as the buttons were stabbed. And it was full of cash. Stuffed full. Every 15 or 20 minutes one of the managers was having to empty it as it became close to overflowing. It never seemed to stop; a seemingly endless gravy (or cider) train. It dawned upon me during that shift exactly how much of a profitable enterprise it must be to have a bar or any sort of concession at Glastonbury. No wonder the demand for places is always greater than the supply and that any traders have to be vetted and to go through a rigorous process before they can set up stall. Which is a good thing I suppose; whilst undoubtedly it is a great cash cow for anyone who can flog their wares, it also gives a sort of guarantee to the paying customers that the stuff they get is going to be, by-and-large, pretty good. (Unless it's chemical grade cider from massive stainless steel tanks, served up in wobbly paper cups for £4.20 a pop. Enough of that for now-I'll have a proper rant about cider later on). But irrespective of alcohol, I've always found the food (and coffee of course) at Glasto to be really good and pretty well-priced. Before we went for the first time, I'd expected it all to be a mixture of crappy vegetarian mush and/or over-priced inedible burgers and hot dogs and therefore fattened myself up in advance. Not that I'd needed much of an excuse for that, but never mind. However, it's good to know that I've never gone hungry at Glasto and it's never cost me a fortune for a meal. The only difficult thing is to decide exactly what to have as the choice is that wide ranging. I cannot fathom out why some people take massive camping stoves with them. I once saw someone cooking a full English breakfast on a contraption that wouldn't have looked out of place on Masterchef. Toast, bacon, mushrooms, beans; the full works. They even had a frying pan with eggs on the go. Who takes eggs to Glasto? Just why? The simple economics of investing in the gear as well as the food must be obvious, let alone the hassle of having to lug all the food around. Tins of beans and boxes of eggs? I always feel like nudging these Boy Scout types, telling them to switch off the gas and to nip over and buy a bloody sausage barm from the myriad of stalls, but they always seem happy with their lot, so who am I to argue?

The shift sped on and I was in my own little world. Phil tapped me on the shoulder and I jumped out of my skin. "You've done an hour and a half on this," he shouted over the noise. (This was the first time I'd noticed exactly how noisy it was, being so preoccupied with keeping the pints going. I'd also not noticed that the music that had been playing over the P.A. had stopped, some band had set up and started hammering some songs out). "Have your break now, 15 minutes and someone can take over from you. You can do the bar when you get back." I nodded some thanks and nipped to the back for a brew and a smoke. Well, I had a smoke first and then made a quick brew. I stood outside, sheltering under some tarpaulin and watched the rain tipple. It was getting darker, but I wasn't entirely sure whether that was due to the fact that it was nearly 8.45 p.m. or that the dark clouds overhead were just getting darker. It was certainly nothing to do with the sun going down. I don't think that it had ever been up in the first place. Those 15 minutes were ticking away very quickly and before I knew it it was time to get back. Steve had just stuck his head round the corner as well, "You ok?" he asked. "I'm fine but that break goes too quick," I replied. "Hopefully, I'll get another one before 12.00 so I can see a bit of U2. Better get back into the fray."

Whether it was down to me being behind the bar, serving the drinks as opposed to simply pouring them, the never ending rain, the racket from the awful band or that something had kicked off somewhere else that was more exciting (hard to imagine) but within ten minutes or so, the massed throngs waiting for their cider dissipated somewhat until it wasn't three deep around the bar with tenners being waved around with reckless abandon. It was busy enough however, to both keep things ticking over and for me to catch up with the band that was still rattling way. To say they weren't much cop was putting it kindly. They were some sort of trip-hop type of thing with a naff DJ and a guitar and bass. Which was pretty ok I guess at a push, but what tipped it over the edge was the singer- who, being a bit of local lass complete with a fairly strong Somerset accent and truly dreadful dreadlocks, didn't really manage to grasp the irony in sounding like a farmer's daughter whilst spitting out "angry urban" lyrics. If you could imagine a cross between the Wurzels and Beyonce with a bit of Massive Attack thrown in, then you'd be getting close. I don't think that it was just me that felt this way as they weren't even noticeable enough to for anyone to boo them. Indifference seemed to be the order of the day. The only applause they got came from what appeared to be a couple of their mates. To most peoples' general relief they soon finished their set and, in the parlance of the day, quickly fucked off. (I think they realised that they weren't very good as they didn't hang around for a drink, but vanished into the night).

As the night wore on and more cider was sold, it became noticeable (to me at least) that people were both more and more dishevelled and more pissed. I think that the two things were connected although the rain wasn't helping with the general dishellevement. Probably what had been a good idea-or seemed a good idea in advance- of wandering around Glastonbury in fancy dress, maybe hadn't turned out as expected after a full days worth of rain and mud. There were more than a few people who looked damp and miserable as they sipped their cider whilst wearing soggy gorilla suits or other such jolly attire. I guess it wasn't much fun stomping around in the mud dressed as Buzz Lightyear or Batman. The irony would have worn a bit thin.

To get to the bar from the metalled path would have normally been a stroll across 30 feet or so of lush verdant grass, or as it happened in 2010, parched, solid-as-concrete, dry-as-a-bone ground. However, as it got closer and closer to 10.00 o'clock and the rain kept falling, we stood and watched what were actually fairly hapless punters negotiate their way through mud that was now at least 18 inches deep. It appeared to have a developed a malevolent mind of its own, trapping people at will and devouring wellies out of sheer, selfish amusement. Lynn and I watched a couple hold onto each other for dear life and take 10 minutes or so to get across these 30 feet (falling over twice and losing a welly in the process).

"It's a shame," she said quite sympathetically, "I feel like waving at them and telling them it's not worth it."

"The cider's shit and over-priced," I laughed, "That'd go down well after all that effort." They finally reached the bar and slumped up against it.

"Yes?" asked Lynn.

"Two pints of lager," he gasped. I did feel a bit sorry for them at this point.

"Erm, sorry", said Lynn. "We only sell cider."

"What? Only cider? Well, that'll have to do. We'll have two pints."

I felt like buying them the drinks myself. Lynn gave them a rueful look when she handed back just loose change out of a tenner.

Things carried in on the same vein for a while. It got quieter and quieter until most of the team were standing around, waiting for punters to turn up, just so we would have something to do. I looked out form the bar and wondered if I could get through the mud and the rain to see a bit of U2 and get back in 30 minutes during my break. This was the plan and after missing U2 the previous year when they'd cancelled I was determined to see them. After all, seeing U2 on the War tour, playing at the tiny Royal Court Theatre in Liverpool was possible one of the best concerts I've ever been to. If they managed to summon up even a tenth of what they did that night then it would have been worth it. I just hoped that my break would happen before midnight. And as if by magic, and to prove the value of wishful thinking, Phil came over to Lynn and me and told us that we might as well take our break while it was quiet. It was 11.00; U2 had been on stage for an hour, hopefully ripping it up good style and still with an hour to go.

I headed to the back of the bar fully intending to head off into the night. As I went to get my jacket, Lynn tapped me on the shoulder."Do you want a cup of tea?"

It seemed rude to say no and I thought I could swig it down quickly and still get off to see Bono and the boys. "Ok, go on then, please. I'm just nipping out for a ciggie." Might as well have a quick one while the kettle's boiling. I stepped out into what I hadn't realised was such bad weather. I couldn't have really noticed it from behind the bar, but it was absolutely bucketing down.

Stair rods.

Cats and dogs.

The whole bag of clichés tumbling from the sky.

I am not exaggerating at this point, but the first ciggie I tried to smoke vanished into the ether. It was if someone had thrown a bucket of water over me. The only way to successfully get it lit and to smoke it was to stick it inside my zipped up jacket and wriggle one of my arms inside. Smoke emanated through all the gaps. If there was ever a time to realise that smoking is a ridiculous thing to do, then that was it. I looked like a soggy parody of Nelson. On fire. Bearing in mind the jacket was nylon based it was a fairly risky thing to do, but if I'd actually caught fire then there would have been no problem. I wouldn't have needed a fire blanket or extinguisher; I could have merely stepped six inches forward into the mud and the rain would have put it out in an instant. The door swung open as I finished my ciggie and Lynn passed me a cup of tea.

"Are you coming in for that or staying out here?" It seemed a bit daft to stay outside so I shut the door behind me and flopped down with the welcome brew in one of the few fold up chairs that was free.

It must have been getting really dead in the bar because nearly everybody seemed to be having their break at the same time; well, at least half of the team. Steve was busy stirring his brew and at least four of the young kids were standing around with cans of Red Bull or some such concoction. (Maybe it was only us old folk that drank tea; I don't know).

"How's it going?" Steve asked me.

"Ok. Well, I guess so. I'm just knackered now I've stopped. How about you?"

"I'm alright, but my feet are killing me."

Lynn groaned and stretched in her chair. "It's my back. My feet are ok, but my back is done in."

Steve laughed. "Look at us. Fit for nothing. We're too old for this. And we've got another three hours to go."

The thought of that didn't exactly fill me with unalloyed joy. A wave of tiredness came over me.

"At least we've got the wrestling to look forward to," Steve muttered, to no-one in particular. That decided it for me. Wrestling would win out over U2. I just couldn't be arsed tramping through the mud, the wind and the rain in what was the twenty minutes or so I had left. Anyway, knowing the way things were going, I thought, I'd probably get there just as U2 would have finished their main set, see them disappear off stage and have to try to get back just as they came back on for the encore. I did feel a bit sort of well, guilty. A few minutes earlier I'd been kidding myself that I was hyper-determined to see them and was put off simply by a bit of mud and feeling a tad sleepy. Maybe I could get there? Maybe I should make the effort? Oh bollocks to it. I had a Mars bar and a banana in my jacket pocket and at that moment they seemed much more of an attraction than seeing the lads from the Emerald Isle; even if they turned out to do a life-changing set. (Which, from all accounts and seeing it on TV when I got home, they didn't). I also had half a cup of tea left to sup.

"I thought you were going to see U2," said Lynn, breaking my day-dreaming.

"Well, I was, but...you know...all this mud and being knackered, they'll just have to get on without me. I did want to see them though. I suppose some things aren't meant to be."

We chatted a while about U2 and I told Steve and Lynn about how good and special they'd been back on the War tour; the sheer energy and excitement that they'd conveyed. Bono climbing up the swaying P.A. tower and jumping across to one of the boxes, nearly breaking his neck in the process; the fact that the theatre had massively oversold the tickets and that it was crammed like the match in one of the old days; seeing a band at that moment when they were on a verge of becoming so big-bigger I think than anyone who was there that night could have possibly imagined; and that however maligned and uncool U2 are seen now, I didn't think I'd ever experience anything like that again. I also told them about the time 18 months before that when I'd missed out on seeing an unknown young Irish band play one night at a small club in Liverpool in front of about 30 or so fans, just because it was on a December night and I was comfortable and warm in the pub. Just like that night at Glasto, I couldn't be bothered walking out into the rain. I hoped that all this wouldn't lead to another lost opportunity. Lightning doesn't strike twice- but you should learn from past mistakes. It was a bit of a dilemma. I just knew that I couldn't tell Amy (yet) that I'd preferred a bar of chocolate and a bruised banana over U2.

"Those 30 minutes went quickly," said Steve as we forced our weary bones back into action and shamble off back into the bar. I hadn't noticed earlier but there was a full size wrestling/boxing ring across from the tiny stage where the band had been playing. Maybe I hadn't seen it because it was that busy, or it was a bit gloomy and dark in that corner. I don't really know how I could have missed something that large but I did. I was fairly sure that it hadn't just been out up in the 30 minutes or so when we'd had our break. I didn't think that there had been much (or any) publicity about it or if it had just been by word of mouth, but there had been a remarkable change whilst we'd been supping out brews. The whole bar was heaving again. This was a very good thing as far as I was concerned as it meant that the remaining few hours would fly by. I could tell that this hadn't gone down too well with the younger members of the team, who generally seemed like they wanted just to arse around all night and not do any work. (You can tell by now that my grumpy old man persona was kicking in; possibly because I was tired or probably because that's just the way I'm turning out to be. This generation's Harry Cross. (For anyone who never watched C4 in the early 1980's, you may have to look that one up). So, in any event, we kept banging out the cider to massed throngs (a hundred or so, but that counts as a throng) who were standing around, waiting for the grappling to start.

If anyone is old enough to recall World of Sport (ITV's Saturday afternoons 1960's/1970's equivalent of Sky Sports) then I expected the wrestling to be a bit like that. World of Sport had a 45 minute slot of wrestling each week, from 4.00 pm to just as the classified football results came in. It was recorded in such exotic locations as Barnsley, Bolton, Croydon, Luton and the like and had to be seen to be believed. I could go on about it for paragraph after paragraph, but that's not what this book is about. Maybe another time. Suffice to say, it is one of those things that, you can look back on and realise that we all grew up in much simpler and more naïve times. I think that sometimes repeats of it are shown on cable. It's well worth catching up on. I didn't expect however, that the wrestling would be like the Las Vegas/WWE American-type glamour fest, all bells and whistles, strobes and pantomime villanry. As the lights dimmed and the crowd's (and mine, to be honest) expectations reached fever pitch, it was nearly time for one of the highlights of the night. I actually may be building this up a bit too much here; after all, if was simply a bit of wrestling and messing about in a little bar. On the other hand, in comparison to the rest of the shift, it was a shoe-in.

There was a bit of shouting and what may be termed a melee on the edge of the crowd. At first I thought it was a bit of a fight. Steve nudged me. "It's all kicking off there," he pointed, and then it dawned on us that it was part of the act. I guess that what wrestling is anyway; not really a sport, more light entertainment. Four wrestling blokes literally grappled their way through the crowd and into the ring. Just like a proper fight, a microphone descended from the ceiling. Not quite like that. I could see someone at the side threading it through one of the ceiling struts, but it had the same effect. They had however, put on a full show. There was an MC, complete with bowtie (and wellies, which sort of was appropriate but odd) and a referee, with one of those black and white striped shirts that American umpires wear. The wrestlers were introduced, in that over-the-top style that you'd expect. I can't recall what they were called, but they were all purportedly from America save for a Mexican who was wearing a face mask and a spangly leotard. As soon as the introductions were over it all went off big time with all four of them in the ring at the same time. They weren't messing around either and although it was clearly choreographed, they did throw each other about in a reckless fashion. The ring juddered under the impacts and there was a lot of booing and cheering from the crowd. From our vantage point it was hard to see exactly what was going on but there was clearly one baddie who relished winding the crowd up and used every excuse to fight dirty. (The words "baddie", "fight" and "dirty" must really be considered only in the context of "professional" wrestling by the way). The Mexican chappie seemed a dab hand at jumping off the top rope and launching himself at his opponents. Unfortunately he also seemed pretty adept at getting himself "whupped", in the quaint American terminology of the evil baddie with the mullet.

We could really only see what was going on over the heads of the crowd and most of that was the aforesaid Mexican jumping around. This spectacle lasted surprisingly for an hour or so. Surprisingly so because all four of the wrestlers didn't let up for a minute. Neither did we, as the cider kept flowing and the tills kept bulging. The whole bout ended with the Mexican "unconscious" in the middle of the ring and the evil villain-who thought he had won- being defeated by the combined efforts of the other two. Which was odd, as a few minutes earlier they had been knocking seven bells out of each other. They were all helped out of the ring, battered, limping and bruised and, like one of those "there's nothing to see here, move along, now" events, the crowd rapidly dissipated, all the fun over.

(As an aside, I nipped out for a quick break and a smoke. Standing at the back of the bar, I heard a few chaps laughing together in very strong Brummie accents. I stuck my head around the corner to see the stars of the show chilling out. Wrestling (like a lot of entertainment) is not what it all seems).

It was now nearly one o'clock and nothing was happening. There were only a very few, very hardy and very pissed souls hanging around the bar. Every so often you caught the sound of brief snatches of conversation; the kind of slurry, intense conversations that only occur when copious amounts of alcohol have been consumed. There was lot of standing around and simply waiting for someone/anyone to decide that they needed yet another paper cup of cider. Every so often the odd person tried to wander through the mud to the bar, found that it was just too muddy and daunting and gave up. I was getting a bit fed-up with it all. The novelty was wearing off and all I wanted to do was to get back to the tent and sleep. Ah! The tent. Would it really still be there by the time I got back? This was a bit of a worry. I leaned on the bar next to Lynn and looked out across the windswept vista. We shared a grimace.

The rain was coming across at 45 degrees and there were rumbles of thunder in the distance. There wasn't much to be said.

"No-one told us it would be like this," she said.

"I know," I replied, "You see all these photos of people frolicking in the sun at Glasto and laugh at the one covered in mud but there's a bit of a gap to reality, isn't there? Your tent going to be ok?"

"I hope so. I think so. It's pretty sturdy." I couldn't say the same for mine, but didn't want to admit it. If it had stood up to the onslaught, it would have been a miracle; it may have even convinced me in a higher power, but that was unlikely. All I could do was to cross my fingers and hope that the rain and wind would die off.

Phil came up to us and asked if, because it was quiet, if one of us wanted to go early. I wasn't bothered one way or another. I didn't fancy trying to get back through the rainstorm and hoped that it would stopped a touch in a bit. Lynn was made of sterner stuff than I, and yomped off as if it was a stroll in the park. Half an hour later, as it reached 2.30, Phil told the rest of us that we might as well jack it in for the night. Steve said he'd hang around for a drink, but like Lynn, I just wanted to get back. In the back of the bar, the snug t-shirt was consigned back to the box and replaced with something more comfortable i.e. my own shirt. I could finally breathe out. Jacket on, ciggies out and lit, second shift over, I headed off back to the tent.

The intense rain of half an hour before had dwindled to a shower, and even that was just in the wind. Maybe things were turning around. As I got nearer towards the Pyramid- and therefore nearer to the tent- I suddenly had an intense craving for a coffee. It had been well over nine hours since I last had one and it had only been cups of tea in the interim. Which were good and all that, but not quite the same. I was betting though at nearly 3 in the morning that there wouldn't be many stalls left open serving food and drink. I passed more than two or three that were closed and in darkness. I was getting a bit twitchy. I just hoped that the urns back at the mess tent would still be switched on and that the coffee hadn't been put away. In retrospect this is not a good sign and possibly an indicator that I'm ever so slightly addicted to coffee. (Excuse me a minute, I must just have a sip of my coffee before I finish this bit. See. QED). As I rounded the corner and headed up towards the hill, squelching my way though lethal puddles and the stickiest mud imaginable, I saw a light shining from a stall. "I bet they're just selling kebabs or something," I thought to myself, "Or they're just shutting up." I couldn't hope for coffee, could I? Not at nearly three in the morning. But not only were they selling coffee, it was only coffee. The only stall that seemed to be open was a coffee one; not a food stall with instant coffee as an add-on, but proper coffee! Things were looking up.

"Are you still open?" I asked. "Yes," said the bloke behind the counter. He seemed Italian, so from a coffee point of view this was a good thing indeed. When I say that he seemed Italian, this was a bit of conjecture on my part. The stall was covered in Italian flags and had Italian colours (red, green and white all over the place). It had an Italian type name, but I can't remember what it was, just that it seemed Italian. The chap was a burly bloke with a big moustache and therefore was Italian. Simple as. (He could have, in reality, been from Preston or Wigan and been a ferret fancier or a massive Rugby League fan, but at that moment it seemed to fit that he hailed from somewhere close to Milan). "Great," I said, "Can I have a big cappuccino please?" "OK, no problem," he replied. (I was slightly disappointed that he didn't respond in Italian and that he had such a good grasp of the English language. I always do have a slight sense of disapproval whenever I buy a coffee and I'm not in England. I feel that I should really only ever drink espresso and that anything with even a faint tinge of milk is seen as wimping out. Pretty sure that's not the case and I'm just being paranoid but there's always that sub-current).

As he rattled away with the coffee, tamping things down and pulling levers, I looked across the Pyramid Field. My God, it was a mess. Glasto have this "Love the farm, leave no trace" thing going on. I don't think that it had quite got through to many people who'd seen U2 that night. Maybe they had seen it-I can't see how they could have avoided it as it was everywhere-but they just didn't care. There was not a square inch of the whole field that wasn't covered in empty cans, plastic bottles or discarded plates of half-eaten food. I am not exaggerating too much at this point. Maybe not every square inch, but certainly every foot. It sends me crazy because it's not as if there's nowhere to put any rubbish; there are bins all over the place and I think that there are so many that it works out a ratio at one bin for every three people. It is sheer laziness that causes people to simply throw their rubbish to the ground; either that, or they just aren't bothered. I suppose they see it as simply as not being their problem and it's someone else's job to clear up after them. It's one thing that makes me both embarrassed and angry. I do think that the attitude is that "we've paid a couple of hundred pounds for our tickets, we can do whatever we like". I feel like turning up at some of their houses and throwing the contents of dustbin around their front room; I wonder how they'd react? Worthy Farm is opened up for tens of thousands of people and it is the Eavis' home and it's treated with contempt. Grr.

I was mulling this over while my coffee was being made. It's always a sign of a good coffee if you have time to ponder. I noticed that the puddle at my feet wasn't being flecked with raindrops and was quite still. It had actually stopped raining. Maybe things were turning a corner. The bloke passed me my coffee and we had a brief discussion about the weather (of course) and how busy things had been; from both a coffee and a cider point of view. I was betting he was as fed up with coffee as I was with cider. It was a great coffee however, and a great chat as well. As I drained the last of the cup-one large cappuccino in less than 10 minutes-and said my good night, he asked me if I wanted another one for the road. (Not in so many words as his English was that good but you get my drift).

"No thanks, "I said "I'm fine."

"Are you sure?" he said, "One last one. You've had a long day. Have this one on me."

Well, I wasn't going to turn down the chance of a free coffee. That's something you don't get every day and maybe a measure of the sort of place Glastonbury is. On one hand, there's inconsiderate bastards dumping their rubbish wherever they feel like and on the other, there's someone offering free coffee. Well, I did take my free coffee, shook his hand and headed off into the night, being very careful not to slip in the mud and spill it all over myself. That would have been ironic.

It was a long and tiring yomp back to the tent, due to a combination of the mud and being generally and totally done in. I'd finished the coffee well before I'd arrived somewhat close to 4.30 a.m. By the time I'd had a long piss due to the coffee and wrestled with the muddy wellies at the edge of the tent; which, to my complete and utter amazement was still holding up, it was nearly five o'clock. I crawled into the sleeping bag and fell fast asleep.

For about an hour. I was deep, deep in the Land of Nod, when the tent suddenly shook, my head was soaked from all the condensation dropping on me. It was if someone had thrown a jug of water all over me. I realised in an instant that something, or in fact someone, had fallen onto the tent. That was it. I was mightily pissed off. "Fuck OFF, you dickhead!" I bellowed at the top of my voice. I heard some muttered, drunken and quite scared apology and the patter, no doubt, of tiny, spindly little student-y legs. It was quite funny. He must have thought that I was some crazed Scouser, ready to leap from the tent, baseball bat in hand. If he'd known that that was the limit of my aggression, shouting a touch loudly, and decided to have a go back, then I may have been in a bit of trouble, being a natural born scaredy-cat. (Oliver Stone's unfinished follow-up to Natural Born Killers; Natural Born Scaredy Cats. U certificate). But the tent was still upright, so he must have been a mere slip of a lad. I grabbed a towel, dried my face, turned over and really fell fast asleep.

Chapter 9

After the Rain

You would think that after all the frantic activity of the day before that I wouldn't have stirred until at least noon. Six hours kip would be the minimum. That's what I anticipated and what I expected when I turned over in the sleeping bag and saw through my half-open eyes that it was bright outside. I fumbled round for my watch. The big hand would be on the 12 and the little hand would be on the 12 as well. The big hand was indeed on the 12, but the little hand was on the eight. "Oh, bollocks to this," I thought, "Eight o'clock. I've only been asleep for three hours. I'm not getting up yet. I'll be dead on my feet by tonight. Going back to sleep." So I wriggled down in the sleeping bag (not the easiest thing to do at the best of times) and closed my eyes.

For about 10 minutes. It was no use. Firstly, I was wide awake and not even in that half-dreamy state. I was completely awake and raring-as much as I am ever-to go. Secondly, it was damn hot in the tent; something I didn't expect with all the rain. I cocked an ear to the side and felt the wall of the tent. I'd either gone completely deaf in the night or it had stopped raining as I couldn't hear or feel the now familiar patter of rain against nylon. And why was it so hot inside the tent and why was it that bright outside? Could it actually be a bit of sun peeking through? I lay on my back with my hands behind my head and hoped that the rain had disappeared for good. That would put a different complexion on things. Finally, and most significantly, I was bursting for a piss. As a relative novice to camping i.e. it was only my second time since Glasto the year before, I was wholly unaware if there were any tricks to avoid this predicament. What I do know now (after the event) is that it's no easy task to get into a pair of muddy jeans, pull a pair of muddy wellies on whilst in a small tent without making everything in said tent become, well, muddy. It's especially difficult to do this with a full bladder. I know this now of course and hindsight is a wonderful thing. But then, it was all a bit of disaster. By the time I'd managed to get my jeans on and sort of twirled the wellies around inside the tent there were flecks of mud everywhere. It looked like some weird Jackson Pollock type art installation, done totally in various shades of brown.

I gracelessly emerged from the tent and slowly stretched my back. I looked up at the sky, squinting at the watery sun like a middle-aged, knackered and slightly overweight Gollum. Yes, that was the sun up there! And although it was still cloudy, they were only those sort of off-white clouds, not the big black evil ones from the day before. Best of all, it wasn't raining. I walked through the mud down to the toilets and thereafter faced a little bit of a dilemma. Now I had had my early morning wee, was I going to go back to the tent and get a few more hours kip straightaway or would the call of a coffee be too much?

I sat by the mess tent with my brew and lit up my first ciggie of the day. There were only a few people wandering around and most of them looked like they'd had a bit of a rough night. From the look of a few of them, they appeared not to have gone to bed at all. One bloke wandered past me supping from a can of Stella, looking quite puzzled in that sort of where-the-fuck-am-I way. I guessed he was going to have a bit of trouble finding his tent. Inside the tent, the breakfast crew were just starting to kick the food off; I could smell the aroma of bacon and sausages wafting through the canvas. This sort of made my mind up for me. I had (albeit not very seriously) toyed with the idea of juts having a quick coffee and a smoke and getting back to the tent for a few more hours sleep. But I figured out that I was only at Glastonbury once and that there would be plenty of time to sleep when I was back home. I also reckoned that a mid afternoon kip might be a good way to go. I could wander around the site in the morning, early afternoon, catch a bit of music, soak up some atmosphere, grab a coffee or two, some carrot cake, see how things were generally panning out and get back at 3-ish for a couple of hours of snoozing. No need to try to get to sleep again at that moment as after a gentle stroll for a few hours I would perfectly placed to drop off. That's not something I could ever do back home on a Saturday afternoon! That was the plan therefore.

With this perfect itinerary in mind I thought I'd better ring home and give Jackie the lowdown on the events of the previous night; as well as getting the latest update on the weather forecast. It was as if I had a direct line to the Met Office.

"Where's my phone?" I thought to myself. I felt round in each of the numerous pockets in my jacket. It wasn't there; must have left it in the tent. Unless I'd lost it. (That's something you'd never hear in years gone by. Can you imagine the conversation in the mid-1970's? "I've lost my phone." "What do you mean "I've lost my phone?" It's here on the telephone table." Can you even buy telephone tables anymore? Did whole factories closed down because the bottom fell out of the telephone table market? Would anyone under a certain age at

Glastonbury know what a telephone table was or even looked like? I remember telephone tables complete with drawer units for phone directories (what are those?) and integral seats (usually covered in an orange/purple/beige fabric). A little shelf for the A-Z phone book (where you wrote down all the important numbers) was a given as well. There couldn't have been anything more 1970's than that).

But my phone wasn't in my jacket. I stomped back to the tent and found it where I'd left it. As this trip of all of 30 yards just to get the phone involved a bit of effort, it called for another coffee.

Nipping back in the mess tent, I could see that a few people were tucking into their breakfasts, although it was generally a lot quieter than the previous mornings. Not quieter in just that there were less people in there, but that the general level of conversation was significantly muted as well. I think that over-indulgence may have played a part in this- there was a universal grey-ish pallor in everyone's faces. I wondered what it would be like by the Monday morning. If it carried on at this rate it would be like eating in a monastery. However, I was possibly doing everyone a disservice. They may have just all been like myself and simply not had a very good nights' sleep. The age demographic of the assorted diners appeared to be at the top end of the spectrum- it could have been that "oh-I-don't-sleep-that-well-anymore" thing that we all drift into as we get older. Anyway, I grabbed my coffee and sat outside to ring Jackie.

It was like having Michael Fish on the line. She is so well organised. She had the browser window open on the BBC Weather page and gave me the update; no more rain, maybe scattered, isolated showers but clearing skies for the rest of the day. Sunday would be sunny and possibly even hot! I gave her a brief lowdown about the events of the previous night-including the near collapse of the tent and the near fight. (Note the use of the word "near" in this context). "You should have chased him," she said. I couldn't explain properly that it would have taken me so long to get my jeans and wellies on that he would have probably been in the next field by the time I'd have caught up with him. The conversation took a bit of a surreal turn as I tried to explain about the wrestling.

"Wrestling? Like what? Wrestling?"

"Oh, I'll tell you all about it when I get back." I promised to ring her later that day, grabbed some breakfast in the tent before it got busy and headed (once again) back to the tent.

Where things had taken a bit of an unexpected turn. Not whilst I'd been either having a coffee, phoning home or breakfasting, but clearly sometime during the previous evening, most likely during my shift. In my knackered state as I got back and in my dozy state in the morning, I hadn't noticed that there'd been a slight leak. My rucksack, which contained all my clean (and therefore, dry) clothes was wet. I suppose it was my own fault as I hadn't covered it up with anything and had left it right against the wall of the tent. A lesson learned in retrospect. Luckily, it wasn't a major leak and nothing else seemed to be wet. There were no standing puddles inside-something that did happen in 2013-and therefore the position was salvageable. With a hint of blind panic, I opened the rucksack and pulled everything out. I had the foresight to have kept all my clothes inside carrier bags inside the rucksack for such eventualities, so I wasn't 100% hapless. The clothes were still ok. Phew. What wasn't ok were all the things I stashed in the little pockets of the rucksack. Boxes of paracetemol, jelly babies, spare lighters; all ruined. Can you imagine how soggy and messy a half-opened packet of Ginger Nuts can get? (I know, who takes Ginger Nuts to Glasto? Squirrels?). Fig rolls, a box of plasters and a couple of toilet rolls also were similarly beyond repair. Everything else was still alright, so after dumping all this stuff in the bin, I grabbed my (dry) towel and headed off for the showers before they got too busy.

Even though it was creeping towards 10.00 a.m. everything was still fairly quiet on the site and no queuing was needed for the showers. The day was starting off well. It was just a bit of a shame that I had to actually do some work that night, but I was two-thirds the way through my shifts and no major mishaps had occurred so far. So far, so good. I managed to get back out of the showers without falling over in the mud and tidied the tent up the best I could. I thought I could get used to this camping lark.

Despite only having just over two hours sleep, I was remarkably chipper. Possibly that was because the rain had stopped and that the sun was warming things through. Maybe it due to the fact that I'd had yet another coffee as well. I was set up and ready to head onto the site. I'd glanced around the mess tent to see if I could see Steve or Lynn, but there didn't seem to be any sign of them. I'm slightly ashamed to say that I actually didn't look that hard; it's not as if I didn't get on with them-they were really nice people- but I just felt at that moment I didn't want to spend the whole day hanging around with people with whom I'd be working with all night. Actually typing this and seeing it in black and white in front of me makes me feel very selfish and embarrassed. Possibly I could have looked harder for them, but I didn't. It was more of a cursory scan around. (As it turned out, they were both still in their respective tents, fast asleep, but I do feel as if I should have made a bit of an effort. Maybe I should have made some arrangement to meet up). However, at the time I was more than happy to have the day to myself, wandering around the site and seeing whatever came up. I went back to the tent, grabbed my little bag for the day (somewhere to carry spare ciggies, bottles of water, phone and should I need it, emergency rain poncho (something I've never used at all at Glasto), and the umbrella, and headed off for a day of, well, general mooching around.

As I headed off through the campsite gate, I could already see that the mud wasn't as bad as the day before. It hadn't dried up at all, but it had lost that evil, catch you unawares, trip you up and yank your wellies off aspect. It had turned less sticky and deeper than before with a consistency of thick porridge. I'm sure that there should be a better way of describing it, but that's how it felt at the time, so I'm sticking with it. It was much easier to get around, although you still had to watch your step. I think that, in retrospect, the whole tiring part of getting through the mud is more to do with having to concentrate all the time rather than the physical effort involved, although I'm sure if I was a bit fitter then I'd have found it slightly easier.

Once I'd swiftly got through the main gates to the festival site itself-having had my wristbands checked and tugged- I then had to decide where to go first. Getting to the Pyramid seemed to be a good starting point. I could get a drink, see what was happening and take it from there. The treacherous pond/puddle/lake from the previous day right next to the gate was still there, albeit slightly smaller and I skirted around its periphery like a seasoned pro. This clearly had not been the case for a fair few others, as there was a mound of discarded wellies about four feet tall right next to it. It was like a monument to the wild and reckless. I wondered how people had managed to get around with only one welly; were there whole battalions of festival-goers hopping around on one leg, or with a welly on one foot and a flip-flop on the other? Anyone who had a stall selling wellies would have made a fortune. It made me more determined to keep mine on my feet for as long as possible. There must be some sort of quasi-military saying that applies to this I suppose, "Treat your wellies as your best friend", or something along those lines. Well, at that moment, those wellies and I were best mates; we were going to stick together through thick (mud) and thin.

Strolling along the tarmaced service road on the way to the Pyramid, I looked up at the sky. It would have been good to see not a single cloud and nothing but blue skies overhead, but that was a bit too much to ask for. The clouds that were still hanging around were wispy little grey efforts and nothing really to be concerned about. It was also warm enough to ditch the jacket, fold it up and stick it in the bag. T-shirt weather had arrived.

Naturally I stopped off at the top of the Pyramid Hill for a coffee and a quick smoke. I didn't have to be quick in reality. That's what is so good about Glastonbury for me and when the penny kind of wholly dropped. I could be whatever I made of it. I wasn't bound by having to fit in with whatever anyone else I was with wanted to do (although, on weighing one thing up against the other, I'd really rather have been having to fit in with Amy's plans if she'd been there). No, there was a distinct advantage of being at Glastonbury by myself. If I wanted to linger over a second cup of coffee or another ciggie, then I could. If I wanted to see a particular artist or band then I could; if I'd been with someone else then I'd possibly have to explain why it would worth walking to the other side of the site to see someone ham-fistedly thrashing a guitar within an inch of its life. That's my sort of music.

On the other hand, there was nothing stopping me from watching two or three songs by an artist and walking away whenever I felt like. I was able to have total freedom of choice. Apart from working my last shift that last night and depending on how the weather turned out, then Glastonbury could be whatever I wanted it to be. I decided to go with the flow and got another coffee.

I could just hear the last strains of Stornaway drifting from the Pyramid. I'd got hold of their last album, played it a couple of times and forgotten about it. A wise move as they didn't sound very memorable at all. I was a bit surprised to see them opening and even playing the Pyramid stage at all. Standing up and peering towards the field I could see that there were only a few hundred punters actively watching them; a general air of disinterest seemed to permeate the area. I wondered who was on next? I rummaged around in my bag and found the small Guardian guide. Flicking through it and squinting at the impossibly small text (it's my age, I know), I worked out that Tame Impala were due to be strutting their funky stuff at ten past 12. This was perfect timing. I could finish off my second coffee and amble down to watch their Australian psychedelic burbling. Or not, if the feeling took me. It was purely my choice.

I'd got hold of the Tame Impala album and quite liked it in a sort of let-it-drift-all-over-me-sort-of-way. I'd played it whilst driving and it was one of those records that either seemed to last a lot longer than you remembered or a lot shorter. There didn't seem to be anything central to it; no type of inner core. It had a whimsical, sub-Floyd, sub-Spacemen 3 feel which was not a totally bad thing. I was interested in how it would come over on a large stage. As I wandered down the still muddy, still slippery but not lethal, hill they were just ambling on stage. I was quite surprised to see that the crowd (of a few hundred or so) that had gathered for Stornaway had, if anything, dissipated a little. This was a band that was highly touted and had received rave reviews. On the other hand, I'd guess that Tame Impala's key demographic weren't really going to up and about at just after noon on a Saturday morning at Glastonbury. It struck me as a bit of an odd billing anyway; I'd have thought that they were more suited to be playing one of the other stages later in the day, but sometimes things work out differently that you'd expect. Not in this case though. I did stay for all their set however and did enjoy it. The whole thing was slightly surreal. Here they were playing on no doubt one of the biggest stages that they'd ever played and they seemed not to be arsed at all. It was taking the laid-back thing to a whole other level. There was a lot of wandering around and switching of guitar pedals, fiddling with amps and long, interminable, guitar solos. I quite enjoyed that guitar noodling as it fitted in well with the weather. The clouds were ever so gradually clearing away and what was a watery sun a few hours previously, was slowly warming everything up. It was if the whole site was on a very low heat. Although it was getting warm for the audience, the majority of us still wearing wellies and hats, I was slightly surprised to see that the band were not following suit. Pandering to my limited preconceptions of Australia and Australians, I would have thought they would have been chilled through to the bone and come on stage wearing sheepskin coats and winter woollies. Probably with surfboards and cans of Fosters as well. (Not really). Not only were they not wrapped up, but a couple of them were wearing sandals and the lead singer was barefoot. This was either taking the hippy thing a step much too far and/or their tour manager was waiting backstage with steaming bowls of hot water for them to put their frozen tootsies in as soon as they got off stage. The whole ambience wasn't helped by an appearance of limited interaction between the audience and the band. The sound was a bit thin and weedy; I think that to have any sort of an effect with this sub-psychedelic sound, it really has to be blasting out and reverberating within your inner organs. It was all a bit, well, tame. But in a perverse sort of way, I really enjoyed it. They did do a very good cover of Massive Attack's "Teardrops" as well. It was good to have the time to stand and watch something all the way though. (It would have been even better if I could have sat down and laid back in the sun. Although that would have been appropriate for their music, I think that I would still have just been swallowed up by the mud). I did read a few reviews of their set afterwards and the consensus seemed to be that they were a bit of let down. It is odd that since then and with the release and subsequent high critical acclaim of their second album, they have become lauded to the skies. Even their live shows appear to be good. Maybe I'd caught them on a bad day. Maybe they'd similarly been woken up after just a few hours kip. They ambled off stage as the set finished in much the same way as they had arrived; a brief nod to the crowd and they were off. A smattering of applause, more out of duty than anything else, rose from the front of the stage and died away as quickly as it had begun. People drifted away.

I didn't really know what do for a bit. The Gaslight Anthem and then Rumer were next up on the Pyramid, both of which I wanted to see. I didn't however, really fancy just standing up in the mud for the next few hours, so I wandered off for a coffee and a sit down. I knew that there were a few stalls nearer to the entrance gates with benches nearby and I worked out I could get there have a coffee and get back before the Gaslight Anthem started. If traversing the site hadn't still been so relatively difficult then I would have had more of a general wander, but at that moment a coffee (and cake) seemed like a bit of a plan. (There will be many Glasto veterans who, at this point, may well recoil in horror slightly at the thought of spending the majority of the day watching acts on the Pyramid and drinking endless cups of coffee. There is an argument that doing such things is a bit lame and not in the spirit of the whole thing- especially as if it's not your first time. I should have graduated to a level of being able to down at least a gallon of cider by noon and then to carry on regardless. Watching anything on the Pyramid is similarly beyond the pale and merely panders to the gross sell-out that the Festival is becoming year by year. Well, each to their own. I wanted to see the Gaslight Anthem and Rumer, and if they happened to be playing the Pyramid, then so be it. And I was sick of cider by then anyway).

It did take me slighter longer to get to where I was going than I expected; not because of the massed throngs leaving after Tame Impala (after all, how crowded can it get with just a few hundred people; it was akin to a busy Accrington Stanley match), but because I'd decided to take the one route that was still fairly muddy and churned up. This being one of the main access routes from an entrance gate to the whole site, I'd guessed that it would get pretty hammered at the best of times and the sheer footfall had meant that the mud hadn't gone away at all.

What did help matters was that there were mini JCB's clearing the really bad mud away into mounds at the side of the path, followed by a tractor, laying down large swathes of hay. This is a measure, a small but highly effective one, of how well the whole thing is organised. The logistics of getting all that gear into the site and crewing it at such short notice must have been difficult, but they did it and it seemed to make a big difference. (This is why it makes me so pissed off when there doesn't seem to be as much reciprocity from those who don't give a fuck and will just throw their rubbish away on the ground instead of using the bins. It doesn't take much effort to do it but a lot of people can't be bothered. I know I've ranted about this exactly the same way only a few pages ago but it makes me very, very cross. And I'm sure I may well mention it again before I get to the end of the book).

It did take me a while to get to where I was going as I passed the JCB and straw combination and ended up squelching yet again. I was heading to what is called the Meeting Place; a handy, well, meeting place. It's a tall sort of tower/signpost thing surrounded by loads of the colourfully painted railway sleeper benches they have all over the site. I suppose the idea of having a meeting place fixed somewhere on site was much more useful in the days before mobiles but even now, it does what it says on the tin; people seem to meet up there. What is best of all from my point of view is that there are many adjacent stalls to get food and drink i.e. coffee and cake.

It had taken me a while longer to get to get there and to be able to sit down with my coffee, piece of cake and a copy of the day's Guardian. (This is very point where shed loads of Glasto vets will shudder in horror and say that I've totally missed the point!) I didn't get much of a chance however to catch up on the latest news from the big, bad world out there as I ended up chatting with the people who were sitting next to me on the bench. Like me, this was their second time at Glasto having been the year before and they were as unprepared as I was for all the mud.

"I think that we were all spoiled by the good weather last time," said one of them. His mate laughed and said that it shouldn't have really been much of a shock that it actually may rain in England in the summertime. They'd come in a group of about a dozen and had a bit of a torrid time; one of their tents had totally collapsed and destroyed with the rain and they therefore now were a bit cramped, although they still appeared to be having a good time. Like talking about the weather and the mud, it always seemed to be a fascinating point of conversation whenever I mentioned what I was doing at Glasto and how I'd got around not being able to get a ticket and it was no exception in this instance. The idea of not having to pay for a ticket in effect always appealed and they all did look slightly jealous when I explained the score re the showers and food. I did temper these positive sides with the fact that not only did I have to work three 8 hours shifts (they seemed to think that wasn't too bad; and it isn't actually) but that by adding the time of getting to the bar from the campsite added on at least another hour or so to the day, thereby wiping out at least half of any day. They didn't seem that convinced and said that they might well think of giving it a go themselves.

"So you'd come again?" I asked.

"Oh, yes, definitely!" they said."Wouldn't miss this for anything!" I wished them luck for the ticket sale in October, finished off my coffee, shook hands (very formal) and headed back towards the Pyramid.

By the time I'd got there (and stopped off to pick up a bottle of water and have a quick toilet break), Gaslight Anthem were in full swing. I think that I'd missed most of their set; I must have done as I only caught two or three songs and they were off. They had gone down fairly well from the sound of things. Loud and pretty rapturous applause followed each of the songs from the crowd, which had swelled considerably from that of Tame Impala. I quite enjoyed them in a Clash-y/Springsteen-y way. (This all too brief review will not go down too well with one of my mates, who is a massive Gaslight Anthem fan, and I'm a bit ashamed to say that I didn't really pay much attention to them. They'd disappeared off stage before I'd really got to grips with them. But as I say, quite enjoyable).

I hung around to see Rumer, who came on stage spot on as advertised at 3.30.The gap between Gaslight Anthem clearing off and Rumer's arrival had allowed me to nip to an ice cream van and go madly wild with a 99. This was a big indulgence as ice creams seem to be the only food at Glastonbury that are overpriced. A bottle of water and a crappy little cone with a stumpy Flake and a squirt of ice cream cost me nearly a fiver. I could have got a pint of cider for less (though not much less). But the significant and telling point is not that I spent so much on a small ice cream but rather that it wasn't wholly inappropriate from a weather point of view. It was sunny and warm enough that having an ice cream was a viable option.

As I quickly polished off the ice cream before it melted in the sun-something I thought that wouldn't have been a concern 24 hours or even 12 hours previously-Rumer appeared on stage and played a very polished set that fitted well with the increasingly relaxed air. It did help that she had a very adept set of musicians backing her, but the songs were just so very good. I know that her album-one of my favourites at the time; and still is now up there for me- is very Radio 2-ish, but I'm at that period when liking music just because it is hip has long gone by.

(Sort of). Still a bit partial to something easy on the ears every now and again. Like Rumer.

I got so heavily into just relaxing and enjoying the Carpenters/Bacharach type vibes floating from the stage that I suddenly realised it was creeping towards 4.30. My plans for a couple of hours of kip before I started my shift would be unachievable. By the time I got back to the campsite, it would nearly be 5.00 p.m. and I'd still have to get something to eat and get back in time for the shift. Maybe I could just catch an hour or so? Would it be possible to do that without just simply oversleeping? I didn't have an alarm clock with me; I suppose I must have had some sort of alarm device on the phone but I didn't have a clue how to set it up. Even if I had an alarm clock, then there'd always be that temptation to turn over, just say fuck it and go back to sleep. No, I thought, I'd best play it safe. No afternoon kip for me. Just plenty of coffee and power through the shift. It didn't really matter I guess about how tired I would be the next day; just as long as I didn't fall asleep in the middle of the shift (always a possibility, but I could blame it on some obscure medical condition). I thought that I should really get back as soon as I could anyway. All the above went through my head in a couple of seconds and just as Rumer was leaving the stage. I didn't exactly sprint back to the campsite, but as a measure of how quickly I wanted to get back, I didn't even stop anywhere for another coffee. I was back at the campsite at 4.55. Crackerjack.

Before I sauntered back to my tent-and as a measure of how much the weather had changed, I could now saunter and at the same time, only need to get to my tent to drop stuff off; rather than check if it was actually still there-I wandered into the mess tent to have a swig of coffee before my pre-meal nap. (I had made such good time back to the site that I thought I could get a half hour in without too much of a risk). As I sat down with my coffee and stretched out my now aching legs, I could feel my eyes closing over. I really needed some kip. Maybe I could just grab forty winks in the mess tent. I was just drifting away when I felt a tap on my shoulder and half-jumped out of my skin.

"Hi!" someone said, a bit too cheerily behind me. It was one of the team who I'd never really spoken much to before. I was very tempted to tell her, politely of course, that I was just about to have a middle aged nap and if it was ok with her, could just give me half-an-hour or so, and I'd be more than happy to have a gab. It would have even been better if she could actually come back in 30 minutes and wake me up, but I thought that was a bit too much of an imposition. I mentally swallowed a sigh and responded in kind, "Hello, you ok?" (I realised then that the dream of having a kip had all but disappeared).

"Yes, I'm fine," she said, as she pulled up a chair, "Do you mind if I join you?"

"No, no, feel free, I'm not doing anything," I said. At this point, I want through that awful moment, when I realised that I had completely forgotten her name. I am terrible with names; I can be introduced to someone and seconds later I have no idea what they are called. It can be highly embarrassing. I was hoping that someone else would join us and solve the mystery, with a "Hi, xxxxx, how are you?" but even then I would probably forget. I am like a goldfish in this regard; a 3 second attention span. I had therefore to stumble through a conversation without knowing her name. This was probably not too difficult but just kind of awkward.

"So, how's it all going?" I asked, "Are you enjoying yourself?" Now she was one of the younger kids in the team, about Amy's age, I'd guess or possibly a bit older. This was the point where I wondered what on earth I could talk to her about, without appearing as some old Dad-type figure. I have no difficulty in chatting to Amy or Thomas or any of their mates, and (pretending) to be being so down with the kids (just to wind them all up) but I didn't want to seem as if I was taking the piss with someone I didn't really know.

"It's really good," she said, "I'm having a great time." (I also felt a little bit guilty after kind of tarring all "the kids" on the team with the same brush in one of my grumpier moments (see a few pages above etc). I probably would have been just the same at their age and I know Jackie would have (rightly) told me off for thinking like that. After all, it could well have been Amy or Thomas that were working there).

So I gave her the benefit of the doubt and asked her all about how she had ended up working rather than just getting a ticket, where she was from and what she thought of it so far. (It sounds awfully rude to keep referring to her as "she" but at that point that's all I could do. I was racking my brain as to remember her name, but it was all a total blank). She couldn't get a ticket-which was like most of us working there I think-but all of her mates and her boyfriend had been lucky. She was the only one out of about a dozen of them who hadn't got a ticket.

"How do you feel about them all having the whole weekend to themselves, while you're having to work?" I asked, "Isn't it a pain?"

"Not really," she laughed, "It's saving me at least two hundred quid and I can get hot food and showers for free!" She explained that she had a tent set up on the site, but that it was just to stow all her gear in; she was sleeping on the main site with her boyfriend and all their mates. Unlike them, however, she was managing to get great food every day, a cooked breakfast and hot showers. She was well fed and clean and they were all caked in mud and cooking noodles on a crappy little camping stove.(Sounded a bit familiar to me). I told her all about Amy and Sacha cooking noodles for breakfast the previous year and about how different it was this time. This was her first Glasto and like many others (including myself), once you've been once you want to keep coming back year after year. I am sure that there are some people that hate the whole Glastonbury experience and never want to go back again, but I honestly have never met anyone who has said that. She was no exception, although she wasn't sure that she'd work again out of choice. Maybe the free food and showers aren't worth it that much.

As I was telling her all about my experiences of getting to Glasto and why Amy wasn't with me this year, I suddenly remembered her name, I thought. I was sure it was Rachel (or was it Rebecca?), something with an R anyway. I was hoping that someone would come along and confirm this thought. I gabbed away about Amy for a bit and realised I was missing her, Jackie and Thomas a fair bit, and wished they were here with me to experience it all.

"You'd never think of getting your Dad to come to Glasto then?" I asked.

"I don't think it's quite his thing," she said, "He's more into classical music."

"Oh, I like a bit of classical music as well," I replied, "But I don't think we'll see much of it here!"

"I've tried to persuade him to come," she said, "But he won't have any of it. He always says "Rebecca, it's a thing for you young ones, and not old folk like me!""

"Oh, just tell him he'd not be alone," I replied, relieved that I'd got her name right and telling myself that I'd better not forget it again. All this chatting had eaten up the time I'd set aside for a nap, but I didn't mind. It was good to discover that not all of the kids working the bar were just there to mess about and hear about someone else's perspective of it all.

"Have you eaten yet?" I asked. She said she'd had her tea, so on that basis, I figured you that she was from somewhere up North (always a good point). I said I was going to get mine as I was starving and she told me she was heading back to the main site to catch up with her boyfriend and mates before the shift started.

"Don't be late then," I said.

"Don't fall asleep!" she replied. (I may have mentioned I was knackered).

I said I'd see her later and went and joined the queue for dinner, sorry, tea.

In a distinctly Northern vein, I polished of a massive plate of steak pie and chips, followed up by sponge pudding and custard. I was well ready for a nap after that, but time had been pressing and it was getting close when I had to do the commute to the bar.

On my way out of the tent, I bumped into Steve, who was rushing in.

"Alright?" I asked. "You're cutting it a bit fine."

"Christ, I know," he gasped, "I got back to my tent this afternoon and fell fast asleep. I've only just woken up." There was a bit of irony for you.

"I'm just going to get something quick to eat, have a quick shower and I'll see you up there," he said.

"I'll tell them you're on your way, if I get there before you," I said.

"Cheers!" shouted Steve over the noise in the tent, as he joined the queue. "See you later!"

It had taken me a couple of days but I had finally got a grip of exactly (or roughly) how long it would take me to get from the campsite to the bar. It would be quicker now that the mud had, by and large, become a lot more navigable. It was either drying up; it hadn't gone completely and was still hazardous in many places, or I was becoming a lot more skilled at getting through it without accident. Of all the things in the world to be able to develop a skill in, and maybe even possess an innate talent, was this it? Being able to get through the mud at Glastonbury? Not for me the ability to learn a foreign language very quickly or pick up a musical instrument. No, the only skill that I have is being able to get through mud in Somerset without falling over. Not very transferrable is it? Not something that I would ever be able to put on a CV with the hope of swinging a dream job. "I have an astonishing knack of being able to walk over a mile in thick mud, whilst wearing wellies and do not fall over. I can also do this whilst smoking and drinking a coffee at the same time if needed." Makes me sound as if I should be in a circus.

Whichever way it was, whether it was all down to my undoubted skills or the fact that the mud was lessening, it did take me much less time to get to the bar. I had gauged it just about right, allowing myself enough time to get through the gates, stop off for a coffee and a smoke at the top of the Pyramid Hill, amble down the hill and skirt round the Pyramid towards the bar. I must admit that that I sped up as I went past the Pyramid. This was solely due to the fact that Paolo Nutini was on stage at the time, complete with his bewilderingly (then) popular faux soft-rock-folk-stompy nonsense. (It is quite instructive actually to look at where some of the artists who have played the Pyramid have ended up. In a not very accurate and completely unscientific type thinking off the top of my head, it seems as if those who generally play early in the day seem to do ok for a couple of year and may even become much more successful. Those who either headline or come on before the headliners are, by default, pretty successful anyway. The real graveyard shift, seems to be the mid/ late afternoon slot (although not on the Sunday "legends" bit, obviously). I'll bet all these artist think that they have finally cracked It, playing the Pyramid at Glasto, but fate has a fickle finger (or something like that).Look at poor old Paolo. Only a few years ago, he was ripping it up in front of thousands at Glasto and now I bet he'd love the chance to be able to get on Daybreak, X-Factor or the like simply to revive his flagging career. (I may be wholly wrong on this point; he may be doing very well, thank you very much. Similarly, the unscientific nature and non-analysis of mid/late afternoon billings on the Pyramid may also be 100% incorrect. It's just a feeling I have). Come what may, I scooted past his set as if my wellies were on fire.

Because my legs had worked so well, I was getting towards the bar a lot sooner than I envisaged. I had about three-quarters of an hour to kill before my shift started. Even allowing myself time to make a cup of tea as well as find the biggest t-shirt I could, then I'd still have 30 minutes or so. I could either go back and catch some of Paolo's nonsense, get to the bar early and have a drink (as if) or see what was going on at the Other Stage. Trying to get anywhere else would have been cutting it too fine. I found the little Guardian Guide inside my bag and saw that some outfit called Jimmy Eats World were probably still on the Other Stage. I'd like to think that I kind of have my finger a little bit on the pulse regarding popular music, but I'd never heard of them. Completely not come across my radar. And this is a bit of a confession and demonstrates how shallow all this musical snobbery can be. Simply from their name alone, I decided that it wouldn't be worth seeing them. It all sounded too 80's-ish; and in a bad way. There are not many linguistic steps between "Jimmy Eats World" and "Johnny Hates Jazz" or "Curiosity Kills The Cat". (I've just looked up Jimmy Eats World on Wikipedia. They are described as American rock. That could mean anything. They may be alright, but I wasn't going to risk it with a name like that). Instead, I pulled by phone out of my bag and phoned home. A much more sensible thing to do.

"Hello? Hello?" It was brilliant to hear Amy's voice. "Dad? Is that you?"

"Yes, it's me! How are you? What are you up to?"

"Oh, nothing. But what are you are doing? How's it going?"

"Mum not told you anything?"

"Oh, she has, but you know, she doesn't understand what it's like there; what IS it like? How are you coping? It's looked pretty bad on the telly."

So I told her all about it; as much as I could anyway over the phone. The camping, the food, the showers, the work, how much I really hated cider now, the music I'd seen and the bands I'd missed, the mud and how hard it had been to get anywhere. How different it all was this year as compared to the previous year.

"Have you been to the Other Stage much? Did you manage to get to Shangri-La? "

"Er, no 'cos of the mud and no to Shangri-La because I was working and knackered."

"Oh you could have gone after work, you know you could," she said.

"I know, I know, but I'm not like you young kids, up all night and partying hard. I need a sit down and a cup of cocoa. And me slippers."

"Hey, I thought you were down with the kids!" she laughed.

"Well, of course I am but I'm more down with the cocoa!" I replied. (It was at this point I really wished that she had managed to get tickets. On the other hand...)

"How do you think you would have coped with all the mud?" I asked.

"You know me," she said, "I would have been dead cobby! I couldn't have all that with wellies all the time and falling over. Just imagine how angry I would have been if I'd fallen over!" She did have a valid point and made me re-think my whole wishful thinking thing. She would have been a nightmare in the mud. A very funny one, but a nightmare nevertheless.

"So what are you doing now?" she said.

"I'm just off to work. My last shift."

"Are you able to see Coldplay later?"

"Hopefully. If I get a break while they're on, I'll try to catch some of them."

"Then you'll get to Shangri-La?"

"Of course I will. I'll text you a photo. Or something like that. Isn't that what you do with phones?"

There was a bit of a pause, then a sigh.

"You are crap."

"I know. Only joking. I really am good with this phone thing, you know. Lol and all that."

"Just be careful if you go there," Amy warned me. (Wasn't this the wrong way round?) "It might be a bit mad. For you."

I promised her that if I went I would be very, very careful, but I think that she (and I) really knew I wouldn't go. After asking for Jackie (who was out, at the shops or somewhere) and Thomas (who was out with his mates), I really had to say my goodbyes.

"I need to save my battery and I need to get to the bar," I said "It was lovely to speak with you. I'll give you a ring sometime tomorrow. Tell your Mum I phoned."

"I will. Have a good night," she said. "And be careful. Love you."

"You too. Bye." And that was that.

I was only a couple of hundred yards away from the bar, but there was a coffee stall right in front of me. Time for a small, quick but refreshing swig-it-down-in-a-couple-of-gulps coffee before I started my shift and got my head around speaking with Amy. It seemed odd going in for my last ever session at the bar. I had only just got used to doing it and it was over. I think that this was the shortest job that I had ever done. And after this shift it would all be over; no more serving cider and no more wearing unfeasibly small t-shirts.

Coffee duly despatched, I had no choice but to go to the bar. I would have loved just to slap it all off and make the most of the night, but work had to done. The evening summer sun was still warming everything through. It wasn't exactly beating down but it gave a gentle, dappled ambience to everything. There were loads of people swanning around, all in various stages of happiness, drunkenness or whatever chemical imbalance they had subjected themselves to. It was all very relaxed. The bar was sort of equidistant between the Pyramid Stage, the Other Stage and the Dance Village. As I walked the short distance from the coffee bar it was quite odd to notice that everyone seemed to be walking one way or another and it was quite easy to spot who was going where. The mid-level Elbow/Coldplay fans heading towards the Pyramid were relatively straightforward to identify, as were the ones swaying their way up towards the Dance Village for a bit of Labrinth and the like. There seemed to be a bit of crossover re the third that would be heading towards the Other stage as the Chemical Brothers were headlining there. I could have spent all evening just people-spotting but I had come this far that I just had to see it all through; irrespective of the fact that if I didn't then the consequences would be expensive. It was that weird sort of last day at school/last day at work feeling. It didn't even matter if I fucked it up tonight, so long as I was there and did my final eight hours.

I bumped into Lynn as I walked towards the bar; literally bumped into her as the crowds heading hither and thither were so crammed. We had a couple minutes chat about what each of us had been up to all day; she had had another wander up towards the Healing Fields and was fully relaxed for another hectic shift.

"Maybe that's what I should have done," I said, "I'm keeping going on coffee and ciggies."

"We've got time for a quick cup of tea before we start," said Lynn "Do you want one?" This sounded like a good idea and I managed to find a large t-shirt as she brewed up.

"It looks busy tonight," I said, as we sipped our teas.

 "I hope so," she said, "It'll go quickly. Have you seen Steve yet? Is he here?"

Although a lot of the rest of the crew were in and milling around, in that way kids do, all hyped to fuck as if they had been ingesting E numbered sweets by the score, I couldn't see Steve. I was telling her all about his late-running escapades as he burst through the door, all flush- faced and panting.

"Am I late?" he gasped, "I've nearly had to run all the way here and it's hectic out there. Don't people know that some of us have a job to get to?"

 Lynn told him that he had about ten minutes to go and passed him a cup of tea. I don't know how she'd known he was going to arrive at that moment; maybe it she was psychic or it was something to do with the Healing Fields and crystals, but she couldn't have timed it better for him.

The door to the bar opened. Phil stuck his head round and shouted for a bit of quiet. "OK, you all here? Good. Right. It's busy at the moment and

I expect it to stay that way all night. Don't forget to i/d anyone you are unsure of. There's a special DJ playing a set later (there was an excited murmur from the young kids at this point) so it should stay crammed. I'll sort everyone's breaks out after. Are you all ok to start in a minute? You know what to do by now. Two of you need to take over the pumps and two of you need to do the till. The rest of you just take the orders. Let's go."

That was to the point, I thought. Bet they've had a busy day.

From the look of it they certainly had. The crew we were taking over from looked completely knackered and couldn't get out of there fast enough. The floor behind the bar was covered in dropped paper cups. Whole sleeves of unwrapped cups had fallen down and been trodden into the mud. It was clear that no-one had time to pick them up. The bar itself was indeed crammed. There wasn't one person standing there who wasn't waving their arms in the air trying to get a drink and desperate for our attention. It was if someone had just called last orders. No, it was more like prohibition had suddenly been announced and was going to kick in in the next five minutes. This was the general tone for the next couple of hours. It never stopped. If I'd thought the previous night had been busy then that had only been a dress rehearsal. But it was great.

There wasn't time to stop and speak with anyone, save for whoever you were serving. The only conversation that you could have was a combination of "How many pints?" "Apple or pear?" " No, we only sell cider," and "Are you 18? Have you i/d?" I tripped myself up re the latter, when I asked one woman for her i/d. This was not a problem and generally anyone over a certain age would be quite flattered by such a question. She was wearing a big floppy straw hat and sunglasses and the low sun in the sky was right behind her, making me squint just to assess anyone, not just her.

"Could you just take your glasses off please," I asked. With a flourish she did so, and I sort of blew any chance of a tip by saying "Oh, you're ok, you're well over 21." Although her friends laughed, she didn't see the funny side at all. I wasn't meaning to be funny or a smart-arse, I actually meant to be reassuring, but it just didn't come out that way. It was one of those (many) instances where I'd put mouth into gear before engaging brain. I had no time however, to ponder my lack of tact and the upset I had caused (she was a bit pissed to start with so I wouldn't have worried anyway),as the person next to her was frantically waving a tenner in my face in an attempt just to get served. It stayed like this for a good while. At one point, Steve looked over to me and grinned. "This is flying by," he shouted "It'll soon be over." I glanced at my watch. It was half nine and it felt as if we'd only just started. Phil had kept everybody on board by making brews for each of us and giving us five minute breaks; just to catch our breath really. A sign of a good manager and I'd bet there weren't many like that. I could see that there was some method in this; it stopped anyone taking the piss and spending ages brewing up. However, it was something he didn't need to do and could have made us all work flat out all night if he'd wanted.

It was during a brief moment having one of these brews that I overhead some drippy kid from London gabbing over-excitedly to Rebecca and another girl about the "special" DJ who would be playing a set later on.

"I can't believe it," he gushed, "This is the best thing ever! DJ Yoda is just so cool."

I raised my weary eyebrows. "DJ Yoda?" I asked "Really?" I had no idea at all who DJ Yoda was. Not the slightest.

"Oh yes!" He was so excited that his voice was rapidly turning into a squeal. "They've done really well to get him to play here. It's marvellous!"

"Indeed," I replied, "Marvellous it is for him to play here." My attempt at a Star Wars reference either fell very flat or more likely, it went straight over his ridiculously coiffured head. There was no time however to debate the finer points of 2011 DJ culture as the few minutes for the brew were up.

He had wound me up anyway. I could put it down to the fact that I was getting tired and that I was getting quite tired, but that probably wasn't the case. He was just a knobhead.

"You'd better get back to the bar mate," I said to him.

"Why?" he scowled, lolling about in the (only) chair that was not broken.

"Well, my two minutes break is nearly up, and you were here well before me. There's everyone waiting for their brew as well." Rebecca and the other girl had already gone back into the bar, but he looked quite settled. I just couldn't be arsed arguing anymore with him. Some people are always dickheads, irrespective. "Oh, please yourself," I said, swigging down my tea and heading back to the bar. He didn't move. "Lazy bastard," I thought to myself. If I was having to work alongside this person for more than the last few hours of my shift, then I would have either grabbed his scrawny neck and dragged him back into the bar or blown him up to Phil. But it wasn't my problem; if he wanted to act like a dickhead, then that was up to him. Everyone else might have been alright with him taking too long for his break; it wasn't really my battle. It was so busy out there in the bar that his extra pair of lazy hands would have made no difference, one way or another. If I took it further then it would have only ended in tears. (In retrospect, and typing all this down now, I think that I really should have tackled him, but hindsight is a wonderful thing).

 So I returned to slapping out fizzy apple and pear juice like there was no tomorrow. In between trying to decipher someone's age from what appeared to be a Finnish driving licence to hearing strangulated cries of "How much?" when I told a bloke he owed me over £25 for 6 pints, it was non-stop. I would have liked a couple of seconds just to say more than hello to Steve and Lynn, but there was no respite. We were all bobbing and weaving behind the bar, trying not to knock into one another as the relentless nature of it all carried on with its own mad momentum. We couldn't pull the pints fast enough. Even though the two machines could each dispense 12 pints a go in a matter of seconds, we ended up with a log jam while we were waiting. I'm glad I wasn't working the pumps on that shift. I was staggered about how much we were serving and how much money was being taken. Even now I look back on it all and think "Did I really do all that? Did that actually happen?" The strange thing is that although it was hectically busy and frenetic, it wasn't hard work per se. It was just non-stop. Maybe this was because it was so relatively simple; sort of any choices you like as long as it's black.

It wasn't like other bars I've worked when you're switching between different pints (lager, bitter, cider etc) and shorts; different glasses, combinations of ice and lemon and a mixture of various prices that you're adding up in your head as you go along. This was easy in comparison. But still tiring I suppose, just because it was busy. I was relieved therefore when Phil started sending the crew on their 30 minute breaks. In some ways it made things easier because there weren't so many people behind the bar and therefore simpler to move around. Less is more and all that sort of things.

As I looked at my watch, I saw it was just after 10.30. If I got my break in the next hour or so (which I would), then I would be able to get along to the Pyramid to see a bit of Coldplay at least. I was still regretting a touch that I hadn't made the effort to try to catch some of U2's set the night before. Was it only the night before? I seemed to have done so much in the last 24 hours. That's the thing about Glastonbury; time seems a bit fluid. Sometimes an hour flies by without noticing and at other times you find yourself saying "Was that only yesterday/ this morning?" Like with U2. So I was all set for Coldplay. A bit ironic that I was actually looking forward to seeing them, and making the effort within a 30 minute break, considering I had been relatively disparaging re DJ Yoda. The lazy, hipster, skinny kid probably would have sneered at me for heading off to see Chris Martin and his merry band of Radio 2 troubadours.

Just after 11.00 p.m., Phil gave me a shout over the constant din, "Do you want to go on your break now?" I didn't need a second thought about that, I was off. (I just had to make sure that I only took half-an-hour; didn't want anyone to think I was taking the piss etc). I didn't even have a cup of tea as I headed through the back of the bar, I just grabbed my jacket and scuttled off into the night.

I had to get my timing right so I wouldn't be late back; for either my shift or to see DJ Yoda. I therefore looked at my watch as soon as I left and noted how long it would take me ; at a brisk pace through the now sporadic mud to get to the Pyramid. It took me 10 minutes; and this allowed me to eat a banana, a Mars bar and grab a coffee on the way. I therefore would have ten minutes of Coldplay. Would it be worth it? Wouldn't it be better just to have a blow at the back of the bar for half-an-hour?

Of course it was worth it. As I reached the Pyramid I was careful not to get sucked too much towards the centre of the crowd, otherwise I would end up being late back. It was packed as far as I could tell, right to the top of the hill. Now I've managed to watch it on TV, I realised what I good gig that I missed. Maybe I should have stayed a lot longer. Certainly they were a lot better than U2 had been the night before. I positioned myself on the right hand edge of the crowd, close enough to see the stage as well as the big screens, but with enough space around me to make a quick getaway.

That previous December I had been lucky enough to nab two tickets for me and Thomas to see Coldplay at the Royal Court Theatre in Liverpool; a venue with a capacity of just under 3000. That was a "hidden" gig with the venue only announced by e mail to ticket holders on the day. It was all in aid of Crisis, the charity for the homeless, and despite Thomas being 21 years old, it was his first ever gig. It was also one of the coldest days of the year. There was thick ice and snow everywhere. We were right next to the stage; right at the very front. The Coldplay gig had interrupted the Royal Court's annual pantomime show for one night only so that all the Panto stage set remained in place as well as Christmas trees either side of the stage. It was truly a magical show. Not just because I was there with Thomas, and not just because we were both so close to the stage we ended up resting out hands on the edge and nearly got our fingers stamped on accidently by Chris Martin's surprisingly large feet; but because we were part of that collective spirit that only happens rarely I think at a gig, (usually only at a small one) when the whole audience are one with the artist and something special and indefinable occurs. (I say indefinable as I can't really define it properly or even at all). But it was special and something I don't think I'll ever forget).

No gig could have been more different to that one than what I saw at Glastonbury. If I held my hand open in front of me and turned to face the crowd up the hill, then I would have obscured as many people as there were in the stalls at the Royal Court (the Royal Court is comprised of three levels; stalls and two tiers).The lightshow at Glasto was like something out of another century compared to that at the Royal Court; it was pure sci-fi. The sound also was, well, just larger and more-stadium-y.

Now at this point, you'd probably expect me to really slag Coldplay's Glasto performance off, for being too stadium-like, too anthemic, too calculated and cold, with no passion and just going through the motions. Much as the way I did with Muse's headlining performance the year before-and, coincidently on the Saturday night as well.

(As an aside, and I'm going incredibly off-topic at this point, but I feel that I owe this at least to my close friends and family; for years and years I detested Coldplay with a passion and contempt that I only held for Simply Red, and latterly (see above), Muse. It was only thanks to a combination of my best mate going on about them, and idly catching a show of theirs on the TV one night when I was bored, that I saw the light. They were so far out of my usual listening habits (The Fall, Dylan and any general tuneless art racket)that shamefully, I had dismissed them out of hand as being boring, without actually listening to them. In the space of just under a year, I had turned from someone who referred to them as Coldpla..yawn into a bit of an obsessive fan. Well, as close as a 50 year-old father of two should turn into fandom without being a bit creepy and odd.)

I wasn't that obsessed as a fan to think that everything they did would turn into gold. I was very well prepared to be disappointed by them at

Glasto and thought that there was a fair chance that they would do a Muse.

I turned up just as they were finishing "Lost". Listening to the recording of this as I type, this was four songs into the set. I stayed for all of the next song, "The Scientist" and once they got half way into "Shiver", I kept looking at my watch and realised I just had to get away otherwise I would be late. (It is at this point when you have probably realised that by referring to the songs just by the titles alone, I am tipping close to fandom. Apologies).

Was it any good? Did they do a Muse?

Yes, of course they were good, and no, they didn't do a Muse. As a measure of exactly how good they are live, they managed to capture exactly the same sort of feeling in that field in Somerset as they did in a freezing, tatty theatre in Liverpool. It didn't seem to matter that they were playing to tens of thousands of people or just a handful. It was still that magical moment. That feeling of connection, of togetherness, of community. Just feeling good. In the space of a few minutes of a song, all the hassle, trouble etc, just disappears. This is what is so good about music. That what it was all about. For all of the planning to get to Glasto, the journey, various debacles re the tent, the mud, the rain, the (very recent) DJ Yoda incident, it was all worth it just for those five minutes of standing there and hearing thousands of people singing at the top of their voices. It didn't really matter whether it was Coldplay in 2011 or The Flaming Lips in 2010. It gave me that Ready Brek feeling inside. So much so that I was even prepared to give old Yoda a fair listening to.

I had to tear myself away from Coldplay (something I never thought I'd write) half way through a song and get back to the bar. I had exactly ten minutes to get back and because I was simply moving through the relatively static crowd rather than being stuck in a shuffling throng I managed to grab a coffee on the way back. This would keep me going for the last few hours of the shift. It did seem really odd that it was nearly all over, and that it would be close to minutes rather than the hours that I'd now be counting down.

As I walked back into the bar, Lynn and Steve were just finishing their break as well.

"Do you know who this DJ Yoda is?" Lynn asked me.

"I have no clue but if it makes these last couple of hours go quickly I'll be quite happy," I said, "You heard of him, Steve?" He shook his head.

"No, no idea. Are you sure it's a bloke? DJ Yoda may be a woman."

"Shows how much we all know," I laughed, "I bet the kids know exactly who he, or I guess she is!" Lynn said that they all seemed pretty excited by the prospect.

So must have been quite a few others because as we got back into the bar itself, it was filling up quite nicely. That makes it sound like a genteel country pub in some small village. "The snug is getting rather full" etc. In reality it was packed with people who could be termed as being off their heads. The cider was being slammed out as rapidly as before. Tills were overflowing with notes. All in all it was quite a good atmosphere; although the fact that I knew it was drawing to a close may have had something to do with it, as well as the afterglow post-Coldplay.

After 20 minutes or so of this frenetic activity, it all stopped. All the punters, like a flock of starlings, suddenly wheeled away from the bar and turned to face the stage. The incessant generic dance music from the P.A. stopped for a brief second. The dim lights went out for a brief moment as well and were replaced by bright spotlights over the stage. There was some off the peg announcement for "a big-up" or something along those lines, for DJ Yoda and the crowd went bonkers. I mentally raised a sceptical eyebrow. I would have raised a literal one, but I've never been good at those Roger Moore-ish expressions; it just makes me look like I've got trapped wind. That is not a good thing at Glastonbury. I nudged Steve. "Here we go," I sighed, "Hold onto your hat."

Well, I was pleasantly surprised at what followed. Not being a big follower of DJ culture in any way, shape or form, I could see that it all made sense (sort of) and was a welcome change (sort of) from watching guitar combos. DJ Yoda himself was not some old wizened green character with pointy ears (although that would have been good, it would also have been too obvious and merely have pandered to my really bad Dad-type jokes); he was older than I expected however, seemingly in his mid-thirties. He manned a couple of record players (or "decks", as I believe the young people refer to them) as well as having a couple of laptops on stage with him. (Maybe he was looking at BBC

Sport as he worked, much in the same way as most of us do while in our day jobs). He also had a few other people on stage who were passing him records every now and then. It was a scene of frantic activity but organised, if that makes any sense. He looked like he knew what he was doing and certainly it was going down well with the crowd, as well as with the kids behind the bar. (I did think that the obnoxious skinny kid might wet himself, he looked so excited). It all seemed to be going a bit over Steve's head; just not his type of thing. Lynn gamely tried to bop along, although it was a bit like a Mum-dance. As for me, dancing, bopping or anything remotely akin to moving to music is never a good idea; I just let it wash all over me. Yoda kept things moving along at a fair old pace, exhorting the crowd to keep it going. Hands were being thrown in the air and people clearly didn't care. (Must have been the cider). Beats were dropped (as the young people etc...) with some aplomb and his selection of tunes was eclectic, but very well judged. There were old swing tunes, bits of Motown, snatches of cartoon and TV clips, splashes of reggae and a touch of scratching. Mixing in Jim Morrison's "stoned, immaculate" speech in the middle of it all was inspired and made me want to hear the original again, something I did when I got home. (Didn't make me revise my opinion of the Doors however, they are still overblown and pompous). The only reservation I had about it all was that it was just too quiet. Not that it wasn't loud; far from it. It was loud enough that you couldn't hear any conversation at all; Steve, Lynn and I communicated by sign language throughout it all. The odd person who actually wanted a drink whilst all this was going on had to do it with a combination of finger pointing lip reading and guesswork. If it had been a bit louder i.e. at ear-splitting levels, then it would have been just right. More would have been more, in an reverse-Zen way. Although I am being slightly flippant, I have to admit that I quite enjoyed it all. It hasn't converted me into someone who will go to Creamfields or the like, but did show me a side of live music that I wouldn't normally have been exposed to. (So for that, many thanks really should go to the Music & Cider Bar).

By the time he'd wound the crowd up to the end of his set, the whole bar was jumping along. (Except for me and Steve). Yoda concluded with a cacophony of beats, strobe lights and lasers and plenty of grins. And that was it, he was off. (As well as most of the crowd, actually). I had only an hour or so left of my shift.

Looking back at it-Yoda's set, that is- two things are apparent. Firstly, we hardly sold any drinks while he was on. Takings must have gone through the floor for those 90 minutes or so. Maybe having him playing had brought some more people in; but they weren't spending much money and I'd bet that he didn't do it for free.

Secondly, and more personally, it did teach me a couple of lessons about music. (Never too late to learn). It is always possible to enjoy something that you'd previously dismissed as worthless or not really something that you'd think you'd like. This I know anyway, Coldplay being a prime example, but seeing and hearing DJ Yoda reinforced it all. What I hadn't fully appreciated until I got home was the power of live music. I'm clearly not talking about live music with instruments here, rather live performances. The overall atmosphere created by seeing and hearing something collectively, as opposed to listening to a CD by oneself, shouldn't be underestimated. Within days of getting back home from Glasto, I had got hold of a couple of DJ Yoda's albums and eagerly stuck them on as I was driving to work, expecting my socks to be blown off. And although I recognised snippets of his set and it was exactly the same sort of stuff that he played that night, it just wasn't the same. It seemed all a bit weedy and premeditated. Better stick to only hearing it at Glasto.

Because the crowd had thinned somewhat i.e. considerably, Phil had let a couple of the kids finish early. I wasn't that bothered, but I could see that Steve was a bit miffed. "How come they got off early?" he asked me.

"Don't know," I shrugged, "Maybe because it's died a death. It's up to Phil I suppose."

"Well, it's a bit unfair," he moaned.

"Why don't you ask him if you can go as well then?" I suggested.

"You don't mind?" he asked.

"No, I'm ok, if can get off, then good for you!" I genuinely didn't mind. It some perverse way I wanted to see it through to the bitter end. I would know that I had done it all and not swerved it off early. Steve did get his early pass and headed off. There was less than an hour to go and there were only a few hardy souls left drinking. Phil came over to me and Lynn and for the first time that weekend, I managed to have a chat with him. It was that quiet that we only got interrupted a couple of times by pesky customers who were keen to carry on drinking.

By the time we'd talked about where we were from, work, family, Glasto, music and the like, it was 3 o'clock and the shift had ended and Phil and the two of us closed the bar. The rest of crew had long gone. Lynn stayed on for a drink with Phil and the two blokes who ran the techie stuff (I wish I knew their names, but I can't remember), but cider being the only choice of drink, and me being heartedly sick of the stuff, I bid them all my goodnights and headed off back to the campsite.

If you have ever see the films *"Escape from New York"* or *"Mad Max 2"*, then you may have a fair idea of what it all looked like as I made way back up the hill past the Pyramid Stage. If you haven't, then it isn't hard to understand what would transpire if a large group of people hadn't slept or washed for 3 days or so and they had largely been fuelled by over-consumption of illegal drugs and/ or alcohol. Fires and cooling barbeques were burning every so often, casting a sort of ghostly atmosphere in the dark night. Every so often someone would stagger in front of me, can in hand, and mutter something indecipherable. I had no time for this. I just wanted to get back to my tent. I suddenly felt very, very tired; which was understandable, considering that I'd only had about 3 hours kip myself in the past 24 hours. And that had been fuelled simply by too much coffee.

By the time I got back to the site, I grabbed one final coffee from the mess tent and sat outside my tent pondering the evening while I had a ciggie. Tomorrow would be another day and with all shifts completed, would be an entirely different prospect. It was with these thoughts in my head that I pulled my wellies off, supped the last of the coffee and crawled, exhausted into the tent. It was nearly four a.m. and as soon as I got into the sleeping bag I was asleep.

Chapter 10

Sunday : A Day of Rest

I'd been in that state of half-asleep/half-awake for a good while-or so it seemed. It was very light outside. I kept drifting off in a sort of keep-pressing-the-snooze-button way for a considerable time even though I didn't have an alarm clock. I heard a few people walking outside the tent and turned over and went back to sleep. I wondered what time it was, but couldn't be arsed trying to find my watch. In my snoozing state, I tried to guess what time it was. I could tell that it was bright and sunny outside. I thought that I should be able to estimate the time by seeing how high the sun was in the sky, in some sort of Bear Grylls way. It couldn't be that difficult. The walls of the tent were that thin that I could see the sun shining through, which was a good thing. It was sunny! That thought alone perked me up. The sun wasn't directly overhead so I knew I hadn't slept until noon but it was at about 45 degrees. Using my newly acquired survivalist skills, I reckoned that it must have been about 10.30, give or take 15 minutes or so. I was so confident in my assessment that when I did finally turn over and find my watch, it came as a bit of surprise to discover that it was still just a little bit after 8 o'clock.

It was quite odd. I was wide awake. Totally and completely. I'd only had about 4 hours sleep; and probably not even that if I added up all the dozing time. All in all, I hadn't slept for more than 8 hours or so in the past 3 days. If I was being utterly sensible, then I should have tried to drop off again and get a few more hours in. After all, it wasn't as if I had to get to work or anything. The whole day was mine to do with as I pleased. But, for that very reason, it was just as logical to get up and make the most of the day. Sleep could come later. And if I was knackered, well, I could always get back and have that much-delayed mid-afternoon nap. It would be my last day at Glastonbury for two years; and that was dependent upon whether I got tickets for 2013, so I'd better make it a day to remember. (But I wasn't thinking about 2013 yet. Not quite).

All these thoughts went through my head in a couple of seconds. The decision to crawl out of the sleeping bag however, wasn't determined wholly upon the application of logic, but something of a more biological nature. I really, really needed a piss. I grabbed my wellies, ready for the inevitable mud-fest outside the tent and made my usual inelegant exit. The sun must have been up for a while, drying up the mud, as the only traces of squelchiness appeared to be isolated to around the water taps and sinks at the bottom of the site. It was still muddy by the tent of course, and although it hadn't dried up enough that I could get to the toilets in just a pair of flip flops, if the weather carried on like this for a few more days, then a repeat of the parched earth of the previous year would surely be on the cards. It was ironic, I thought, how much a few days difference in timing would have made to it all.

I half-toyed with the idea of getting back in the sleeping bag after my comfort break, but I knew I wouldn't. The coffee was calling me from the mess tent.

I was sitting outside the mess tent, coffee and ciggie on the go, in my now usual spec (it is funny how quickly habits form) and was just about to ring home when one of the Glastonbury support blokes pulled up in his buggy thing and asked me for a light.

"How's it going?" he said.

We got chatting, somewhat inevitably, about the weather. Apparently we were all due a scorching hot day. 27 to 30 degrees.

"Really?" I said, "Where did you hear that?"

"It's what the BBC are saying," and with that he showed me his phone. It was the BBC -so it must have been true- there wasn't a hint of cloud at all on their graphics. "This is why the cart's full of water," he said, pointing at the cases on the back. "We're trying to stock up everywhere with as much as we can before it gets really busy."

I guessed that he was a fair bit older than me; and that's saying something. He was a big bloke with a bushy beard and didn't look like someone you'd mess around, but we ended up chatting for a while.

We talked about how it had all gone this time, how busy it had been and of course, all about the mud. He said that it took a good six weeks to get everything back down again; the fences, the tents, metal roads but when it was all done, it was like a normal farm again. "I love working here," he said. "Best job I've ever had."

"You must have had a few," I replied.

"Oh aye, I've done everything but this is the best one by far. I've been doing this for fifteen years now and it gets bigger and better every time. You know what the best thing is about it?"

I shook my head.

"Every year it's different. Not just the weather, but different to what you are expecting. You can never guess what it'll turn out like."

"I suppose it was very different before the fences went up?" I asked.

He laughed. "You never came back then?" I wished I could have said I was too young, but I don't think he would have believed me.

"No, last year was my first time. I came with my 18 year-old daughter and her best mate. Wish I'd done it earlier but..."

At this point he climbed down off the buggy and pulled up a spare chair. He was obviously going to relate a well-worn tale. I offered him a ciggie as I had an idea we would be there for a bit. I had read of, and knew I thought, of what happened before the fence went up, and why it went up, but it was interesting to hear it from someone who had been there at the time. It was fascinating. He gave me a potted history of the festival, from its early roots and how it started, through to mad days of the fence -jumping through to when the big fence finally went up, and right to present day.

"I don't think that anyone imagined at the start that it would have gone on for so long," he said, "In fact, every year we thought it was going to be the last one. Especially just before the big fence went up. That was nearly it. The Council and the Police really wanted it all stopped. They were looking for any excuse to stop it all. So that's how we ended up with this fence. If it wasn't for that, well, we wouldn't be sitting here now."

I said that it must be expensive.

"Oh, it is," he said, "but it's the only way that the Festival could have carried on. So its money well spent, I reckon." I offered to go and get him a coffee, but he said he really needed to get on, "These cases of water won't deliver themselves. Nice to talk with you though-see you next year?"

"Oh yes", I replied "I'll be back."

"Good man."

We shook hands and he climbed back on board the buggy, waved me goodbye and chugged off though the gates.

After all that, it really was time to get like E.T. and phone home. (I've been trying to get that in for ages). I had been talking and listening (more the latter than the former) for the best part of 45 minutes. I did need a coffee however, and nipped inside the mess tent. I noticed that it had filled up quite considerably whilst I'd been gabbing. It wasn't as if there weren't any spare tables or seats, but it was far from as empty as it had been before. I was quite surprised by this, it being Sunday morning and all that Sunday mornings usually entail. Maybe it was a combination of people wanting to make the most of their final day at Glasto or just getting their breakfast before their shifts started. Phoning home would have to wait. I thought I'd better have something to eat before all the food ran out. Just a couple of slices of toast would suffice. That's all I needed.

It's not what I finally ended up with of course. (You didn't think I'd only have that? After all, it was going to be a busy day-the food was free and whatever I had was going to have to keep me going all day). So a large bowl of Sugar Puffs and a full, full English breakfast was duly despatched. It was time to make the phone call. Actually, I was more than ready for a kip after such a large breakfast. It was getting that sunny and hot that I half-contemplated heading back to the tent, opening up the camping chair for the first time that week and slumping down in it, hankie on my head and trouser legs rolled up, 1950's Northern/Blackpool sunbathing style. But I didn't have a hankie, it wasn't very sandy and there wasn't a donkey hanging around.

"Good morning!" said Jackie, "And what time do you call this?"

I looked at my watch. It was nearly 11 o'clock. I hadn't realised that I'd spend so long talking and having my breakfast that it was nearly dinnertime. Or at least elevenses.

"I've actually been up for ages," I said, then with a sudden comprehension that I could be digging a bit of a hole, "but I, erm, got chatting to some bloke and had my breakfast and didn't realise how late it was." I filled her in with all the exciting events of the night before-Coldplay, DJ Yoda and the rest. She told me about everything that had been going on back home. Amy was out and Thomas was still in bed.

"I'll ring up later and speak with them then," I said, "Anyway, what does the weather say?"

Jackie confirmed exactly what the bloke had said; hot, getting hotter and sunny, getting sunnier. I don't think that was exactly the words that the Met Office and the BBC had used, but that was the general gist of it all.

"So what are you going to do with yourself all day?" she asked.

It was a good question. I hadn't much of a clue.

"I'm not sure. Just go for a wander around and see what happens."

"Are you going to see Beyonce later?" (Jackie asked this more in the sense of was I going to watch Beyonce headline the Pyramid, rather than nip backstage for a pre-arranged meeting, a cup of coffee and a slice of carrot cake with Ms Knowles and Jay Z). I had quite forgotten about Beyonce playing, but I didn't think I'd go and see her. There'd probably be something different and better on one of the other stages.

 "I don't think so," I said, "I'll see who else is playing. There's plenty of choice. I do want to see Paul Simon this afternoon though; he should be good. I'll plan everything out later."

"Well," she said, "I've recorded everything that I can from the TV so far. Coldplay looked brilliant!"

That made me determined to see as much as I could during the day, rather than just odd bit and bobs. "Right," I said, in a things-to-do type-way, "I'm going to get a quick shower and work out a plan of action. I'll phone you later. Bye!"

Luckily, there was no queue for the showers and as the clock ticked closer to noon, I was back by the mess tent, ready to go. I had a couple of bottles of water, three bananas and the only packet of biscuits that hadn't been soggied out in the flood in my bag. I was optimistic enough regarding the weather and the mud to also have my fold-up chair to hand (not very rock and roll, but quite frankly, I'm past all that). I even threw in a tube of sun cream and my cap; something I didn't think I'd need a mere 48 hours before.

I flicked through the Guardian Guide, wondering who and what to go to see. It was quite a novel experience; without having to do a shift I could pick and choose whatever I wanted. I tried to work it around the ones I wanted to see; Paul Simon was on the Pyramid at 4.30 and Robyn Hitchcock was at the Spirit of 71 Stage at 6.30. (I am not an especially big Paul Simon fan it must be said; I have one Greatest Hits compilation and a ripped copy of Graceland, but I thought that the weather would fit well with some big hits and most of Graceland). Simon and Hitchcock apart, I was kind of torn between artists I really thought I should see and those that might turn out to be good, Duane Eddy was on West Holts at 5.00 and TV on the Radio were playing the Other Stage at 5.30. Eels were on the Other Stage at 7.00 but Plan B was on the Pyramid at 6.15. Everything seemed to be clashing. I decided just to play it by ear and see how it all went. Still didn't know how I'd end up the day; was it going to be Beyonce or not?

As I was pondering all these choices and finishing off my coffee, I saw Lynn shuffling towards the tent. She didn't look too spicy.

"Hello!" I shouted and waved at her. She sort of jumped out of her skin. "You ok?" I asked, "Didn't mean to startle you."

"Oh hi" she replied, "I'm feeling a bit fragile this morning. I had a few drinks last night and I've only just got up."

"I suppose you'll have to head to the Healing Fields later on then?" I said.

She laughed, but in that sort of quiet way you have to when you have a hangover. "I probably will do, but I'm just going to get a coffee and go back to my tent. Have you see Steve this morning?"

"No, no sign of him, but he finished early last night, so maybe he's already up and about."

"You look like you're ready to go as well," she said, pointing at my chair

"Oh aye," I replied, "I'm going to make the most of the day, Can't spend all my time sipping coffee!"

"That's what I think I'll be doing," Lynn said, holding her head, "I feel so rough."

I stood up and hoisted my bag over my shoulder. "Looks like you need to sit down for a bit," I said and passed her the chair. "

Thanks," she said as she sat down, "I think I'll just sit here for a bit."

"OK, then, you going to be alright?" "Yes, I'll be fine, I think. Going to pass on the coffee. Just going to sip some water and get some more sleep."

"Right," I said, "Maybe I'll see you later. Take care."

"OK. Bye. Have a good day. See you later."

"Bye!" And I was off, leaving her to nurse her hangover.

As I headed through the gates and onto the main site, I thought to myself that it would be so good just to have the whole day to do with what I wanted and not have to work. Part of that was pure selfishness I supposed. It had been good to have someone to chat to whilst I'd been working, like Lynn and Steve, but as I said before I didn't really want to hang around with them when I wasn't. I was able to see whatever artists I wanted to and go wherever I felt like without the need for keeping other people happy. This does sound a bit harsh as I type it and it's not meant to. I'm pretty sure that they may well have not wanted to hang around with me as I drank endless coffees and watched hapless, relatively inept indie bands trash at guitars to waves of indifference.

It is different I think, when you go with someone you know, like I did the year before, with Amy and Sacha. Then I could put up with having to watch The Cribs and they could stand and see the Flaming Lips with me. We were also in a position to go and do our own thing if we wanted, but could get pissed off with each other (which actually happened surprisingly rarely) and let off a bit of steam without too much upset. For instance, Amy could tell me off for moaning and being miserable and I could nag her about wearing enough sun cream. I was also at hand to check out the toilets for them in advance and they knew me well enough to treat me to an ice cream when I was flagging. You can't do that with people you don't know that well. All in all, I was quite content to be spending the day by myself in the sun. (It would have been better if Amy, Thomas and Jackie were with me, but there would always be other years).

Walking past the gate I was staggered to see what had been a veritable lake a couple of days before had disappeared, leaving a simple patch of rapidly drying mud. I even thought about nipping back to the tent and changing my wellies for my, as yet, unworn boots but I didn't really know what it would be like once I got into the main site and I couldn't be bothered with the trooping back. Once I was on my way that was it.

One of the advantages of having a staff wristband was that you didn't have to always go through the main routes onto the site. This meant that I could skirt along the back of the hill in relative isolation then drop down to the Pyramid without having to struggle through crowds and crowds of people. The only things I had to watch out for as I walked along the tarmaced service road were tractors and waste trucks. I could hear the music drifting up the hill but just as loud as that was the sound of birds twittering away in the hedge that ran alongside the road. It made me wonder what exactly it was all like when the festival was over and everyone had gone home. It would be great just to wander around and listen to the wildlife. With a start I realised that I was turning a bit hippy-ish. One more step along this route and I'd be wearing crystals and heading towards the Healing Fields. It was time for a ciggie and a coffee. And some loud music.

Which I probably wasn't going to get by watching Don McLean on the Pyramid Stage. I think that like most people there, the only songs of his that I knew are Vincent and American Pie. I don't especially like the former and as for the latter, well, I know its sacrilege to even mention this, but I prefer Madonna's version much more.

So whilst Mr McLean was standing on the Pyramid strumming and warbling away as most people used it as an opportunity to go somewhere else, I was sipping a coffee and pondering my next move. I'd missed Alberta Cross at the Other Stage which was a bit of a shame as I fancied a touch of thrashy rock. I couldn't be arsed with anymore of Don's singer songwriterly introspection however, and I wasn't going to hang around to see the folk-tinged affectations of Laura Marling who was on after him. Braving the crowds, I headed down the hill towards the Other Stage. (It wasn't exactly a crush getting through because of Don. The hardest thing was negotiating my way past everyone else who had the same thoughts as I had i.e. get away from it all as fast as you possibly could).

On the way to the Other Stage-I decided to head in that direction simply at random- I stopped to pick up a copy of the days Observer. After all, it was Sunday and some traditions must be maintained. I knew that keeping in the spirit of Glasto, by now I should have really been on my third or fourth pint of Cider and if not pissed, then fairly glassy-eyed. But it was the paper for me and a cup of coffee. That would do just fine.

As I headed past the Music & Cider bar, I very nearly popped in to ask for a pint of lager, just for old times' sake. Actually, Phil had said to me the evening before to nip past and have a drink. If he had been there, then I think I would have done, but I didn't recognise any of the team that were working and the only bar manager I could see was the narky one I'd been warned about. (I hadn't worked with her at all during any of my shifts, hadn't seen her around the site apart from the first day and didn't really want to make her acquaintance then). I therefore strolled briskly past, newspaper under my arm, like some deranged commuter with my wellies on my feet. It did look fairly busy; I was so glad that my time there had ended. I did however, fully intend to nip back sometime later that last day for a brief drink. It would have been rude not to.

I'd tried to get close to the Other Stage sometime on the Friday, but it was so mud-ridden that it was impossible. Even a tank couldn't have got through. On that Sunday afternoon it was a totally different matter. Although it wasn't at the levels of baked hardness, like an evil cricket pitch, as in 2010, it had dried up remarkably fast. There were people actually lounging on the ground and not disappearing without trace! That decided it for me. The chair would come out and I'd have a pleasant sit (and maybe even a nap) for an hour or so before heading back to see Paul Simon.

I ended up close enough to the stage to see just about what was going on but far enough away that I could unfold the chair and stretch out without getting in anyone's way. It wasn't that busy anyway and there was plenty of space around me. Alberta Cross must have finished their set; there was no-one on stage and it was that state of limbo before the next act came on. I sat down with the fullest of intentions to skip through the paper; see what was happening in the big wide world outside, catch up on the sport and the like. Before I did that however, I pulled my wellies off, wriggled my toes and pulled my cap down. I would "just rest my eyes" for a few minutes. I wasn't going to drop off, oh no; too much to do and see. I'd just have a deep relax.

I was gone. Fast asleep. I don't know if I'd been snoring or drooling, but I was far-off in The Land of Nod. It must have been a combination of the sun, the ending of the shifts and basically not having had more than the equivalent of one night's sleep since I'd first arrived. Whichever way it was, I was completely gone. It wasn't a nap or light doze or any of that type of sleep that you have when you half-asleep and half-awake and therefore have a vague notion of what's going on around you. I could have been anywhere. Someone could have run off with my wellies, the contents of my bag or my hat I wouldn't have stirred. I could have been the chair robbed from underneath me and I think I still wouldn't have noticed. It was brilliant. The best sleep I have ever had.

I don't know what exactly made me wake up. It may have been due to the next band coming on stage, someone actually trying to rob my chair, a drifting odour wafting from the toilets near the Other Stage or some subconscious feeling that I really shouldn't be fast asleep in the middle of a field in Somerset in the middle of a Sunday afternoon. Whichever it was, I woke with a start. One of those waking-up moments when you sort of jump yourself awake, if you know what I mean. I am unsure if I shouted or grunted in my sleep which made me wake up. I do have a habit of talking in my sleep, so that was a distinct possibility as well. (On one occasion, I talked that much in my sleep that I managed to Jackie everything that I'd got her for Christmas and I never knew a thing about it until she confessed to me on Boxing Day). There was therefore always a chance that I'd been talking gibberish at the top of my voice while I'd been asleep. However, I don't think that anyone would have paid much attention to me. They'd have probably thought I was pissed or stoned. Anyway, I did have a quick look around to see if any was staring or pointing. Or laughing. And for a moment I had that strange sort of dislocation that you get when you can't figure out where exactly you are. Had I fallen asleep at home and was I dreaming that I was at Glastonbury? Was it…all just a dream? No-one was looking at me. Everyone was just wandering around as per usual.

As I slowly came round, I realised It wasn't a dream. I looked up to the sky. It was as cloudless and blue as it could be. The ultimate summer sky. Nothing that felt this good could be a dream. It was all too real.

I shuffled up in my chair and stretched. I was properly awake now and ready for the rest of the afternoon. I'd only been asleep for about half-an-hour or so, but maybe that's all that I needed. There was too much to see and do to waste any more time napping. Besides which, I really needed a drink and something to eat. I was properly peckish. What to eat? Where to go? I was spoilt for choice. It would seem like a bit of a pain to have to uproot myself from my settled spot, fold up the chair and gather everything back together again (bag, paper, wellies etc). If there had been many more people around, then I'd have just asked them to keep an eye on things while I wandered over to get some grub, but it seemed as if most people were just wandering around between acts and using the space as a bit of a thoroughfare. It only took me a second or so to anyway to grab everything and go foraging.

Fifteen minutes later I was back in the same spot, unfolding my chair and settling down for a bit of dinner. Wellies back off, large coffee by my side, big fluffy slice of pizza and a strawberry muffin so large that it should have had a sticker on the side stating that it could serve 4. Paper unfolded and sun belting down. Now this was the way to go. As I took my first bit of pizza, I got the oddest sense of déjà-vu. It was something I couldn't put my finger on at first. It wasn't even that déjà -vu feeling initially, but more of a unsettled feeling, as if things were not quite right. (It was nothing to do with the pizza by the way, which, without turning this into a food review, was absolutely perfect). Then the déjà-vu kicked in when I realised that I was eating exactly the same stuff, on exactly the same day, at the same stage and sitting at what must have been virtually the same spot as I had the year before. I wondered if it had been merely co-incidence that had brought me to this or if had been something subconscious. Whichever way it was, this year I was sitting by myself and not with Amy and having a laugh and a chat. In what was probably the only time while I've been at Glastonbury, (or even the only time ever), I suddenly felt homesick. I wished Amy was with me, pinching bits of my pizza and messing about. This was a time just to hear her voice. I switched my phone on and called her up. Knowing Amy, I bet her phone had either run out of charge or was switched off, but no, she was actually there.

"Hello?" she said, "Dad, is that you?"

That was all I needed. Simply to hear her. It may be a cliché (well, I know it is) but it was a ray of sunshine. The homesickness had gone and everything was back to normal.

"Yes, it's me. How are you?" "I'm ok. What are you doing?"

"You'll never guess what I'm doing," I said. (I think in retrospect that I may have been over-egging it at bit at this point. Amy was probably expecting me to tell her that I wangled my way backstage and was hanging out (I think that the expression the kids use is chillin') with Beyonce). When I told her actually what I doing and where I was she did sound more jealous than impressed.

"Oh, I wish I was there right now," she said.

"So do I," I replied, "I'm in exactly the same spot, I'm sure, that we were last year. Not the same though, eating a pizza by myself."

"I bet," she laughed, "Me and Sacha aren't pinching any of it off you!"

"It's great, I can have all of it, without bits disappearing!"

"What are you up to next?" she asked. I said I wasn't sure what to do for the rest of the day, but that I'd just have a wander round and see what happened.

"Are you going to see Beyonce tonight then?"

"I dunno. Not really my cup of tea but.."

"Oh you really must. She'll be amazing! There's things on the net saying that Jay Z or Coldplay might be on stage with her. Have you heard anything about that?"

I said I hadn't but that I'd keep my ears to the ground. After chatting a bit more, finding out that everything was fine back home and that she was alright, we said goodbye and I promised her that I'd ring her after I'd seen Beyonce that night. (I wasn't intending to see Beyonce, but I thought I could blag it). I got back to my pizza and coffee in a much improved state of mind. After all, as Amy had said, next time it would all be different. We'd all go together next time.

Pizza finished, I was ready to start on the muffin. The other thing that was due to start was the next band on stage. The Noisettes. Someone who I think I had heard of but not actually heard, if that makes sense. I had no idea what they were like; although I feared that they would be some sort of Cribs/Vaccines-guitar-Brit-pop nonsense. In the words of the song, should I stay or should I go? Being pretty relaxed at this point and as I had some coffee left, I thought that I might as well give them a go. At least it would give me something to write about later on. There were also quite a few more people heading to see them and settling down and they didn't exactly seem like a beered-up Brit-pop crowd. A older couple sat near to me with their chairs and what seemed to be a quite remarkable picnic basket. It looked like a day in the park for them. I don't know how they managed to prepare all the food that they laid out on their travel rug, but there was everything you expect with a full blown picnic. Sandwiches, pies, sausage rolls, salad, cakes; the lot. You don't get people bringing picnics along for The Cribs, I thought. I wonder what this lot would be like?

And on that summer Sunday afternoon they were very good indeed. From what I remember they seemed to be a sort of retro-60's Soul type thing. Full of tunes and extremely cheery indeed. I would have got up and had a dance if I'd been so inclined. Probably not. I don't really do dancing but it was enough to get my socks wiggling along as I flicked through the paper and finished off my dinner. It all went down very well with everyone that was there as well, as far as I could see. Smiles were breaking out all round and a good sign of anyone going down well at Glasto is when the flow of the crowd is more towards the stage than away from it. I suppose that the palpable air of happiness was due in some way to the improving weather and that it really had turned out to be a perfect summer afternoon, but I'm sure that the type of music The Noisettes were playing had something to do with it as well. I resolved to get some of their stuff when I got back home and give them a listen. I never have however. Maybe it would have been similar to cooking something back home when you've got back from holiday and it not just tasting the same as it did when you ate it under Mediterranean skies. So from that afternoon to this, I've never heard The Noisettes again. I think that it's better to leave them as a perfect memory of that afternoon; falling asleep in the chair, chatting with Amy on the phone, eating pizza in the sun and having a piece of cake from someone else's picnic.

I wasn't like Yogi Bear. I didn't come up with a cunning plan to pinch someone's picnic basket. Although, if Amy had been there, then she would have made a perfect Boo-Boo. No, as I was enjoying the music in my own little world, I felt a light tap on my arm. It was the woman with the picnic who was sitting next to me.

"Hi!" she said. "Would you like a piece of cake? We've brought too much with us and it seems a shame for it to go to waste?"

"Well, if you're offering!" I said, "It all looks very nice."

And indeed it was. You can't beat a slice of fruitcake while gabbing away to people you've never met before. Yet another thing that is special about Glastonbury. Complete strangers offering you cake (certainly something I'm not ever going to turn down) and spending a hour in good company, talking about the whole experience and more. I don't think it could have happened anywhere else.

By now, time had clicked on however-it was well past 6'oclock- and I did really want to get to see Robyn Hitchcock at the Spirit of 71 Stage. I said my goodbyes and thanks to the picnic people (bad with names again), folded my chair up and headed off. As I reached the signpost directing me towards the Spirit of 71 Stage and struggling through the crowds, which were getting busier and busier, I had a change of mind. I just couldn't be bothered trying to get there. It was a bit of a hike after all and I'd had, in retrospect, such a good afternoon that I didn't want to spoil it. I had a fixed plan to watch Robyn Hitchcock, but weighing one thing up against the other, I decided to head on back to the tent for an hour or so. Recharge my batteries and make a start on sorting stuff out. I was sure that I'd get to see Robyn Hitchcock some other time, if not at Glasto, then when he next toured.

It felt quite liberating on the way back to the tent. I could have gone to see Robyn Hitchcock but decided for fairly arbitrary reasons not to. Just because I could.. These decisions are easier to make when you are by yourself; maybe not always the best ones, but if it goes wrong then you can't really blame anyone else. As I wandered slowly back through the site, stopping off for a coffee near the Meeting Place, I tried to take everything in. This would be the last afternoon for a couple of years that I'd be meandering back to a tent. There is just so much happening all the time at Glastonbury that it's so easy to miss out. Although this was only the second year that I'd been, and I hadn't (purposefully) seen that much, I think that you could go for decades and still only scratch the surface. There is such a wide range of people, all there for the same reason and yet all there for different reasons. I can't recall ever hearing anyone saying that they haven't enjoyed it or that they've hated the whole experience; I'm sure that of the 180,000 that are there every year, then there must be some who'll never go back and have had a miserable time, but I'd bet there aren't many. Certainly everyone who I've ever spoken directly to about it, love it to bits. There seems additionally to be a common thread amongst those (like myself), who having been once, question why they didn't make the effort and go earlier.

Tied very closely with that is the next question; will we get tickets for next time? Will we be lucky?

There is already that faint sense of a panic about the following year, I think, on every Sunday afternoon/evening every year. You can feel it in the air. "Will I be back next time?" Maybe it leads to an odd mixture of sadness and recklessness? I wasn't feeling very reckless myself; nor very sad it must be said, although it did cross my mind as to whether or not I'd be able to get tickets for the next time. In two years! What a long time to wait! I determined not to think too much about that. It would only lead to questions of whether I'd work again if I couldn't get a ticket and at that moment, sitting in the sun and watching the whole, diverse Glastonbury world go by. Work was the last thing I wanted to think about.

I was in no particular rush and I think it must've taken me an hour or so to get back to the campsite. By the time I'd half heartedly tided up the tent -this consisted of throwing away anything that I didn't want to take back home and what I didn't need that night (I must stress at this point that although I did throw stuff away, I did put it in the correct bins and most of it was simply rubbish)-and phoned home and spoke to Jackie again (who was still trying to convince me to watch Beyonce), then it was time for something to eat. The last meal at Glasto for a while. The Last Supper, so to speak. (There was always breakfast the next morning to consider. At this juncture, I think that this book may read simply about what I ate and how much coffee I drank at Glastonbury. There was more to it than that. But not much more really.)

I wandered into the mess tent and looked around. It was all fairly quiet. I didn't even recognise anyone in there and for a second I wondered if I'd walked into the wrong tent. The only folks I kept my eyes open for were Steve and Lynn and they didn't seem to be around. Hopefully I could catch up with them some time before it was time to go. I supposed that most people were either doing their last shifts or were making the most of their last day, and not spending time eating a full meal.

However, I was made of sterner (i.e. greedier) stuff than that. After all, it would be a while before I'd have another hot meal. I strolled up to the counter and plumped for fish and chips. That would do. Apple pie afterwards. Perfect. As I was finishing the last crumbs of the apple pie and still browsing through the paper, I noticed Rebecca wandering over to me with a tray full of food.

"Oh hello!" she said, "How are you?"

"I'm ok," I said, as she sat down. "What are you doing here?" I asked, "I thought you'd be on the site with your boyfriend and all your mates ripping it up, now that your shifts are all finished."

"I have been!" she said, "But they've all run out of money and I'm starving! I thought I'd get a meal back here and take some food back for them. Besides, I had to come back to sort my tent out."

I said that it seemed like a good plan and asked exactly what she was going to take back for them, seeing as it would be a bit tricky to both con extra plates of fish and chips out of the catering crew, let alone carrying plates across the site.

"Oh, I scrounged a couple of loaves out of them and some pasta and that should keep everyone going until tomorrow." She showed me her bag. There were two loaves crushed together as well as a carrier bag full of cooked pasta.

"Doesn't look very appetising," I said.

"They're all pissed," she replied "They'll eat anything!"

Well, I thought to myself, that's kids for you. Been there, done that etc. But the lure of a proper plate of food counts much more for me. We had a brief chat about what we were up to that evening-she would be doing all the dance-y field stuff and I said I still was unsure, but that I was kind of toying with the idea of seeing Beyonce. (Just for the want of saying that I was doing something. It just seemed a bit daft to say that I didn't really have much of a clue). As I'd finished my meal and time was ticking along I decided to give Thomas a ring to see what he thought about Beyonce. If he went along with Amy and Jackie then I'd go with that. I said therefore said my goodbyes to Rebecca and wished her well for the rest of the night.

"See you later," I said as I headed for the door of the tent. (I don't know why we all actually say that when we know that it is very unlikely we will see someone else again. Maybe it's just too impolite to say the opposite).

"Hello Son! How are you doing?"

"I'm alright Dad, what are you up to?"

"Well, here's the thing." (Thomas and I had just watched the whole of The West Wing series and I had been looking to use the phrase "Here's the thing" for long time). "

What do you mean "Here's the thing"? You are not a Deputy Chief of Staff in the White House!"

"I know, but it's cool and I got to use it before you!"

"So what is the thing then?"

I explained that I was in two minds really about going to watch Beyonce and I really needed him to make my mind up for me.

"What other options have you got?" he asked.

By now I'd walked back to my tent and was just unfolding my chair.

"Hang on a sec," I said, "I'll just tell you how it pans out."

I plonked down in the chair and rummaged through my bag. I squinted in the sun at the small type on the Guardian guide. It was either the sun shining so brightly or (more likely) the fact that my eyes were getting worse as I get older. But it was hard to read it.

"Well, it's either Beyonce at the Pyramid, Queens of the Stone Age at the Other Stage or The Streets at the John Peel Tent. What do you think?"

"I don't know," he said.

"What would you see?" I asked, "Not what do you think I should see, but if it was you what would you go for?"

"I don't like The Streets at all. I think he's a knobhead."

A fair, yet pithy critique.

"Queens of the Stone Age? They're a bit naff are they? A bit metally?"

Again, correct on both counts.

It should be said that for both Amy and Thomas, music doesn't play such a significant part of their or their friends lives as it did with mine or my friends at their age. Or even now. Maybe it's something to do with the ready availability of music, its sheer ubiquity, or just possibly they've got more important and relevant things to do than obsess about music. They are possibly the first generation where their musical tastes are more inherently conservative than their parents. However, it has to be said that by a process of aural osmosis over the past 20 years, my offspring have are now able to tell the difference between The Fall, Captain Beefheart and Blind Willie McTell. They may not actually like any of them, but they do know what they sound like. And because of all this, and even with a limited interest in things musical, Thomas was rightly indentifying two crucial elements. The Streets were knobhead-y and QOTSA were a bit metally. There is nothing worse than being a bit anything as far I'm concerned in respect of music. It's similar to buying a bottle of water with a hint of lime or something. It should either be a bottle of water or a bottle of lime juice. The same applies to music. No point in having a hint of metal; just play proper metal music. Nothing wrong with that. Even play something different with metal elements- but anything that can be a "bit genre-like" is homeopathic nonsense.

"So?" I said, leaning back in my chair and almost toppling over, "That just leaves me with Beyonce then?"

"So there's nothing else on any other stages then?" he asked.

"Yes, but.."

There was nothing really more to be said on that point. I think I had convinced myself.

"I'll have a look but probably go and see something else," I said, "She's all a bit show-bizzy for me."

Music duly dealt with, we talked about football for another 15 minutes or so, how things were back home and how much I was looking forward to getting back into my own bed. I said I'd ring them all later and let them know how I'd got on with the evening entertainment.

I still didn't really know what I was going to do that night. I suppose if I had been there with someone else then that decision could have been taken out of my hands, but as it was, it was all down to me. Time was really ticking on and whatever I was going to do, I had to do it soon. As I had to really walk close to the Pyramid wherever I was going (not really but it kind of went that way), I decided I might as well have a glance at the Vegas-fest that would be the Beyonce show. I could then always pop off to catch something else.

It felt better once I had determined what I was going to do. It was time to move. I decided not to take the chair with me; after all, that would be a step too far down the OAP route on the last night at Glasto I folded it up and lashed it in the tent, grabbed my bag and headed off towards the site.

It was just hitting 9.00 pm as I went through the gates. The sky was turning dusk on what had been a brilliant day. Quite naturally, I stopped at the top of the hill for a coffee and a ciggie and surveyed the scene laid out in front of me. It is a magical place. Not, I think as I said earlier, for me, all the ley-lines and crystal-type magic, but quite simply the sort of place that makes you realise you'd rather not be anywhere else in the world at a particular moment. In those ten minutes or so while I had a smoke and sipped my coffee, it grew darker and darker and dusk slipped into night. I looked across the site and saw the lights twinkling for what seemed miles and miles. What could be better than this, I thought to myself. All the mud and rain and worry about the tent blowing away and the hours spent serving shit cider seemed a long, long time ago and not just a few days earlier. Now the June sky was clear as crystal and the faint sparkling of stars was echoed by all the lights all over the site. It had all been worth it.

As I sat there pondering and musing on such thoughts, I slowly noticed that more and more people were heading past me and onto the Hill. I hadn't expected that much interest in Beyonce. I anticipated that there wouldn't be much excitement about Pendulum who were on before her; I caught the very last few minutes of their very last song, but only drifting towards me in the air as I reached the coffee stall. I don't think that I had missed out on an earth-shattering performance. I thought that if I was going to get to see a glimpse of Beyonce then It would be advisable to get a better viewing spec, although I'd need one quite near the edge of the crowd so I could beat what would no doubt be a hasty retreat. I supped my coffee off and wandered down the Hill. I did think about getting another drink but I could get one on the way to see someone else. I'd only be there for a couple of Beyonce's songs. I ended up halfway down (or up) the hill, facing the centre of the stage, but with enough space around me to head back up and away. I looked around at the people near to me. There were a group of three women, I'd guess in their mid to late thirties, all ready to dance along to Beyonce. Standing with them was one bloke, who I took to either be a long-suffering partner or an extremely grumpy looking stalker. As much as they all looked to be up for Beyonce, he was at the opposite end of the spectrum. He fitted every cliché of a chap being dragged along to the shops on a Saturday afternoon while the match is on. Apart from them, the rest of the crowd appeared to be a fairly mixed bunch and certainly not what (in what must be admitted, was my somewhat blinkered and slightly snobbish predetermined view), a demographic close to the usual stadium tour audience.

The lights on the stage dimmed and the crowd grew restless with anticipation you get either at the match as it kicks off or at a large gig such as that one, I sighed the sigh of a confirmed cynic. "Here we go," I thought, "Viva Las Vegas."

Then...BLAM!!!

The opening notes of "*Crazy in Love*" started very slowly as blue strobes illuminated the stage and Beyonce stood silhouetted in front of a large white triangle, singing the first lines of the track. The blue lights turned into a swirl of bright white and then, as the song kicked in, fireworks shot high into the sky from either side of the stage and it all turned bright red. "Glastonbury?" she asked "Are you ready?" There was a massive shout from the crowd and it all kicked off. I have been to some loud gigs before i.e. Killdozer in the mid 80's, yet this was something else. I just know and understood that this was largely pulling all the Las Vegas'y type strings but bollocks to that; this was just utterly fantastic! I definitely wouldn't be heading off anywhere while this was going on.

It was all spectacular, but not in the throw as much as you can at it a la Muse or some rock bands, where you know that it is all utterly false, insincere and premeditated, but genuinely spectacular in a sense that it takes your breath away. Of course it was premeditated, because it was so good and well put together. It was premeditated in a professional, rehearsed way rather than in a cynical manner. It was that difference between doing something with care and respect and love for the audience rather than with contempt. I have been to many, many gigs over my increasingly advanced years, from tiny shows at little clubs with unknown bands to stadium gigs with "megastars", to, of course, Glastonbury. Hand on heart, I can honestly say that I have never, ever seen any performer at any time create such an instant and deep bond with an audience as I did watching Beyonce at Glastonbury that June evening. I have never seen anyone have such a sheer *command* of a stage. It wasn't down to all the pyrotechnics, the swirling ever-changing light show or the incredible volume, It wasn't down to the incredible quality of the songs or the unbelievable tightness and precision of the all-female band. It wasn't the brave construction of the set-list; which kicked off with two of her biggest hits, Crazy In Love and Single Girls- always a risky step starting with your two best songs- but she took it on and took it higher. There was something else; something indefinable. You could have taken all of it away and it wouldn't have made any difference. That Beyonce gig was the best performance, and really therefore the most unexpected performance, that I have ever had the privilege to observe. And that is the word-privilege- that I think best describes it all. I was just so lucky to have been there that night.

I'm not sure if the bloke standing close to me would have agreed 100 per cent with me, but three songs in, he unfolded his arms and nodded in to me in a sort of "well, we may be blokes and we're not really supposed to like this, but it's ok really" sort of way. I felt that he was a more of a QOTSA type-he looked like that anyhow. On the other hand, the three women were getting into it in a big way, singing along and dancing like loons. I was closer to him, outwardly; tapping my wellied toes and humming along at odd moments was as exuberant as I get, but inside I was bopping like an elf on meth. Or something like that. It would make a bit of sense to run through the set, track by track but that would just be a list of songs. I could pick out some highlights, but the whole thing was highlights. Let me just pick a couple to demonstrate how special it was.

A cover of Prince's "*The Beautiful Ones*" segued into Kings of Leon's "*Sex on Fire*". Now, it must be said I love Prince and have seen him live, but "*The Beautiful Ones*" isn't his best or most memorable tunes. In the hands of Beyonce and her band; those musicians and that voice, well, it transformed it totally. It was if the song had been given wings and allowed to soar. I'd have never have guessed that any Prince song could be improved or indeed, made it sound as if the little one had held something back, but that's what she did with that. The Kings of Leon. Let's face it, they are slightly shit aren't they? "*Sex on Fire*" is an ok song though. Possibly the only good song they ever did, yet it is hackneyed and overplayed beyond belief. You'd never think that could be sound fresh and powerful. That's what happened at Glastonbury in the space of a couple of minutes. The penultimate song that she did was "*Run the World*". I said that the gig started with her strongest and best songs. It did, but this one came a close third. I think that by the end of it the QQTSA chap was convinced. Certainly, like virtually everybody I could see, he had a massive grin on his face, and the effects of Beyonce's music had caused his grumpiness to totally evaporate. As for me, a few hours before when I was unsure about watching Beyonce, I would have never expected that it would have turned out the way that it did. Of all the things I saw at Glastonbury that year, then that was the single 90 minutes that I really wished Amy had been there to share it with me. If I could have bottled up that feeling of happiness that was almost palpable in the air by the time the gig had finished and take it home, then it would have kept me going for a very long time indeed.

Sometimes you're at a gig and even if it's good, you find yourself glancing at your watch every so often. Not in this instance. The hour and a half flew by. It was astounding. I thought she'd only been on stage for 30 minutes or so and before I realised it, she was drawing the whole thing to a close. It was nearly midnight and it was nearly all over for another year.

Well, two years actually. Crap.

(In case you may think that I that I'm over-hyping everything and that it wasn't that good actually, or that it was a result of a lack of sleep and/or some subconscious attempt to end the week on a high, that thought has crossed my mind a couple of times as well. I have however, the benefit of watching it all as broadcast by the BBC ripped onto a DVD, as well as an audio recording. If anything, I've underplayed it. Even a couple of years down the line and hundreds of miles away, it is still as powerful. It goes to show that having a closed mind about music (or anything) is not a good thing. You never know what is just around the corner).

It was all over. I could have wandered around more of the site; I should have, looking back at it all now, wandered around for a bit and seen what was going on elsewhere. (That was something I did manage to do, and made an effort with in 2013. But that's another story altogether). In my defence, I was knackered and the Beyonce show had been that good that anything else would really have taken the gloss off it all. These are pretty lame excuses, I know. For anyone who's been to Glastonbury before and reading this, you'll surely be thinking that I had hours and hours worth of stuff left to do. All the reasons about being tired are rubbish really; I could sleep plenty on the coach on the way home and besides, surely I'd drunk enough coffee to keep me wake until the following morning at the very least. Hindsight is a wonderful thing however, and I just didn't think things through properly.

Still, as everyone wandered off to wherever they were going; back to their tents, somewhere else on the site (exciting and thrilling no doubt) or just back home, it was hard to escape the odd mix of unalloyed joy about what we had all seen and the slight sadness that that was kind of it. An ending of course, but a good one. People were shaking hands and hugging; sharing drinks and laughing and big smiles seemed to be the order of the day (or night, I suppose). Even the QOSTA bloke turned around to me and shook my hand.

"That was alright wasn't it?" he said.

"Pretty blinding," I replied.

"Er, see you next year," he said, "Got to go and keep up with those three." He pointed towards the women he was with who were already heading down the hill to pastures new. "Bye!" And he ran down to catch up with them.

I went in the opposite direction and towards the campsite. As soon as I found an empty bench to sit down on, I switched on my phone and rang home. I hoped that someone would still be up.

"Well," said Jackie, "Did you see Beyonce?"

"Of course I did! I wasn't going to miss that! What did it look like in TV? Did you see it?"

"Oh, it was brilliant! I recorded it for you. Did you see the fireworks at the start? It looked really packed. Wish I'd been there."

"So do I. Did Amy see it?"

I could hear Amy in the background shouting away. "Tell me Dad he makes me sick!" I took it that she had watched it.

"What are you going to do now? You going on anywhere else? " asked Jackie. (She'd never been to Glasto and even she knew that I should have gone on elsewhere).

"I'm heading back to the campsite. I'm knackered. I'll ring you in the morning. See you tomorrow. Love you."

I slowly sauntered back to the campsite, taking my time and taking everything in. I walked a long way round and it was nearly half past one by the time I walked into the mess tent. There were only a few people in there; one group had a collection of cans and boxes of wine in front of them and were, I would suppose, somewhat over the drink-drive limit. Apart from one couple who were nestled in a corner and deep in some earnest conversation, that was it. I slipped in and made myself an quick, and last, coffee. I stood outside my tent as I finished it off and listened to all the mix of sounds gently floating up from the site in the clear, summer night sky.

Nowhere else quite like it.

Chapter 11

Time to go home

Just like the last day of a holiday, when all you want to do is get to the airport and get back home as soon as possible, because you can't really do anything on your last day of the holiday and there's no point in hanging around, that's how I felt as soon as I woke up on the Monday morning.

No, it wasn't really. I didn't want to leave. I did want to get home and see everyone again, but I didn't want the whole Glastonbury experience to be over. I wondered if I could sort of stowaway and hang around Worthy Farm like a phantom for the next couple of years. It would save me all the hassle of having to get a ticket.

I knew that I'd have to get home however and back to work and all that entailed. I turned over in my sleeping bag and looked at my watch. It was just after 7 o'clock. I could tell that outside the tent it was shaping up to be a marvellous day, weather-wise. The coach was picking us all up at 9.00. This gave me two hours to get some breakfast and pack everything up. I wriggled out of the sleeping bag and poked my head out the tent. I expected the site to be a hive of activity, but it didn't seem to be any busier than normal. I supposed that many people were leaving it to the last possible moment to make a move.

But as I was awake, I thought that I may as well make a move. Better get some breakfast while I could and before all the food ran out. I didn't really want to be left playing a metaphorical breakfast pass- the-parcel and be the one left with the bowl of All-Bran at the end. I fumbled around the tent, grabbed my ciggies, threw my jeans and wellies on and remarkably exited the tent with some sense of style. It had only taken me nearly a week to be able to do it. No-one was around to see it and bearing in mind I would be taking the tent down in the next hour, it was kind of ironic.

I'd smoked my first ciggie of the day by the tent I'd got to the mess tent and thankfully the breakfast had just started being served. Just like the site, there weren't many people around so I managed to get a full English down me. Within half an hour I was sitting outside the mess tent with a coffee and a ciggie and watching people come and go. I was hoping to see Lynn and Steve somewhere along the line, but as I didn't know where their tents where I wasn't going to start roaming the whole site on the off chance of bumping into them.

I made a quick call home and checked that Robbie was still ok to pick me up from Sheffield. At least he would know the exact route this time. Another coffee in and there was still no sign of either Lynn or Steve. They would be on different buses than me, so maybe they weren't getting picked up until later. It was time for me to pack everything up anyway. I figured it would take me some time.

Back at the tent I surveyed the scene and made an instant decision. The tent was fine but I don't think it would last packed away for another 2 years. Besides, next time I would be there I wouldn't be alone and therefore would need a bigger tent. My sleeping bag (which had cost peanuts) was covered in mud and ripped at one end, the airbed was leaking (there had been a gentle hiss all through the final night. That was definitely the airbed rather than myself as it was flat as a pancake). One of my wellies had split along one seam; it was lucky that all the mud had dried up. It therefore took me all of ten minutes to stuff the sleeping bag and airbed in one bin bag and the tent in another. I pulled the tent pegs out of the ground and threw them in another bin bag with all the other rubbish, including my wellies, which had stood by me well all through the festival. I stuck my boots on for the first time in days; it felt very odd. I then took the three bin bags to the bins and all that was left was a flattened patch of grass to show where I had been. I picked up my rucksack and the chair and took them to the gate.

But I had an hour or so to kill before the coach would turn up. I could have sat in the mess tent drinking coffee for an hour-why change habits?-but on a whim, decided to head on to the site for one very last time. I could get to the top of the Pyramid Hill and back well within an hour. It would be interesting to see what was going on. There was a steady stream of punters heading out and home through the gates, but I think I was the only person going in the opposite direction. As I walked through the gate, I managed to snaffle one of the full Glastonbury glossy A4 programmes for nothing, instead of the usual £12. It would be something to read on the way home.

Ten minutes later, I reached the top of the hill and looked across the whole site. The early morning haze was burning off and it looked like it was going to be a beautiful day. I could have stayed there for hours, just watching all the coming and going. I'd picked up a last coffee from one of the only stalls still open and sat down on the grass. Idly, I looked at the programme. The back cover had a single shot of the very top of Pyramid Stage, with the sun setting behind it. In plain white typeface, superimposed across the centre of this photograph, it read "Glastonbury 2013. 725 days and counting..."

The journey back was quite uneventful. I think it was, although I couldn't be exactly sure as soon as the coach reached the motorway I was fast asleep. The only time I woke up was when there was a scheduled motorway stop at a God-knows-where service station. Everyone piled off the coach headed into Burger King or KFC for 30 minutes and got back on again. I think that there were a few who didn't even get off for that, but remained in a catatonic state all the way back to Sheffield. The coach was certainly a lot quieter on the way back than on the way down. It rolled into Sheffield sometime in the late afternoon. Everyone disembarked and headed off their separate ways. Surprisingly, Robbie was waiting for me exactly where we had arranged to meet. We managed to miss the rush hour traffic past Manchester and I was home by tea time.

Jackie was waiting. "The kettle's on," she said, "Do you want a coffee?"

Epilogue

A lot of people asked me what it was like working at Glastonbury rather than going as a punter and hopefully this book has explained, in part, how it was for me. The other questions that people ask me are if was it worth it and would I do it again. These are a bit more difficult to answer and maybe I've only touched upon them by implication. I think that the way it was for me was clearly shaped by the fact that I was a) by myself and b) considerably older than the vast majority of the crews working there. I am sure it is very different if you are in your early twenties (I can vaguely recall being that young) and with a group of your mates.

As to whether it was worth it; well, despite that a large chunk of your time is spent working and therefore at someone else's beck and call, if it is a stark choice between going to Glastonbury in any way possible or not, then of course, for me, it is worth it. And therefore, faced with such a dilemma again, I would work it. No questions asked.

But did I work it in 2013 or did I get a ticket? Did I even go? What do you think?

Of course I went!

THE END

Acknowledgments and thanks

Thanks must go to Glastowatch for all the information on the Glastowatch forum; it is really invaluable for anyone who is going for the first, second or umpteenth time to Glastonbury.

Everyone who has posted helpful advice on the Glastowatch forum must also be thanked; especially Glastoworker whose advice and information provided much needed reassurance before I started serving pints.

I would also like to thank Glastowatch for tweeting links to "Turn Left at the Womble". Without that I'm sure that many people wouldn't have picked up on it. Eternally grateful.

Many thanks to Gary and Dave for publishing "Turn Left at the Womble" through Twitter as well as to everybody else who has re- tweeted it.

I have changed some of the names in the book; apologies to anyone who didn't get their name changed. That was purely by chance and due to my poor editing.

I should also thank everyone I met and talked with at Glastonbury. It's the people who go there that make it what it is.

I can't forget all my family and colleagues at work for hearing me rabbit on and on about Glastonbury. I suppose apologies are in order.

Final thanks must go to Michael and Emily Eavis. I doubt that they'll ever read this book, but if they do, I owe you both a huge debt of gratitude for making your home and place of work such a special place.

,

Printed in Great Britain
by Amazon.co.uk, Ltd.,
Marston Gate.